Eastern
Great Lakes

INDIANA • MICHIGAN • OHIO

By
Thomas G. Aylesworth
Virginia L. Aylesworth

CHELSEA HOUSE PUBLISHERS
New York • Philadelphia

3   5   7   9   8   6   4

Library of Congress Cataloging-in-Publication Data

Aylesworth, Thomas G.
    Eastern Great Lakes: Indiana, Michigan, Ohio
Thomas G. Aylesworth, Virginia L. Aylesworth.
        p. cm.—(Discovering America)
    Includes bibliographical references and index.
    ISBN 0-7910-3409-7
            0-7910-3427-5 (pbk.)
        1. Lake States—Juvenile literature. 2. Indiana—Juvenile literature. 3. Michigan—Juvenile literature. 4. Ohio—Juvenile literature. I. Aylesworth, Virginia L. II. Title. III. Series: Aylesworth, Thomas G. Discovering America.

[F551.A95   1995]   94-37217
917.7'09692—dc20   CIP
                                                AC

CONTENTS

OHIO

Indiana

The Indiana seal, officially adopted in 1963, has evolved from the original territorial seal designed in 1801. It is circular, and shows two trees in the left background and three hills in the center background, with the sun shining between the first and second hill from the left. On the right are two sycamore trees. In the foreground are a woodsman with an ax and a buffalo jumping over a log. Surrounding the circle is "Seal of the State of Indiana" and at the bottom, the date 1816.

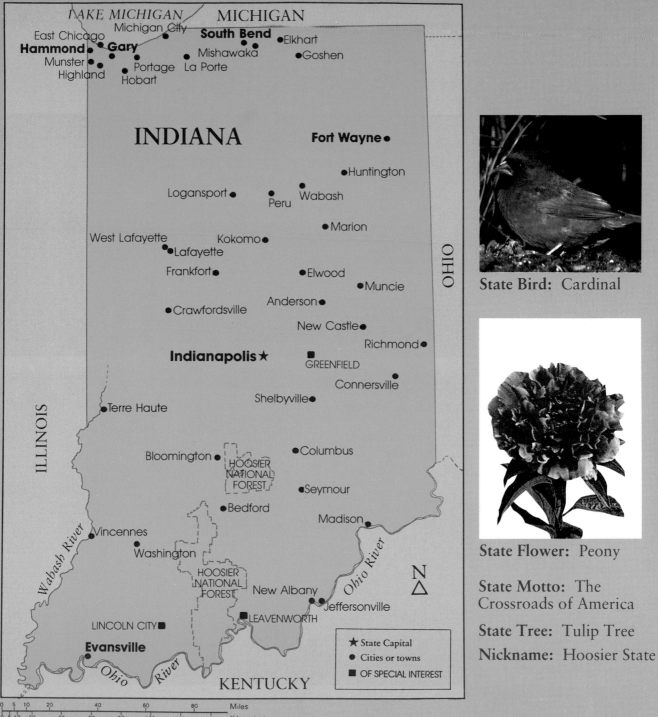

INDIANA

LAKE MICHIGAN — MICHIGAN

East Chicago
Michigan City
South Bend
Elkhart
Hammond — **Gary**
Mishawaka
Goshen
Munster
Highland
Portage
La Porte
Hobart

Fort Wayne

Huntington

Logansport
Peru
Wabash

Marion

West Lafayette
Kokomo
Lafayette

Frankfort
Elwood

Muncie

Crawfordsville
Anderson

New Castle

Richmond

Indianapolis ★
GREENFIELD

Connersville

Terre Haute
Shelbyville

ILLINOIS

OHIO

Bloomington
Columbus
HOOSIER
NATIONAL
FOREST

Seymour

Bedford

Wabash River
Vincennes
Madison

Washington

HOOSIER
NATIONAL
FOREST
New Albany
Ohio River

N
△

LINCOLN CITY
LEAVENWORTH
Jeffersonville

Evansville
Ohio River

KENTUCKY

★ State Capital
● Cities or towns
■ OF SPECIAL INTEREST

0 5 10   20   40   60   80   Miles
0 5 10 20   40   60   80   100   120   140 Kilometres

State Bird: Cardinal

State Flower: Peony

State Motto: The Crossroads of America

State Tree: Tulip Tree

Nickname: Hoosier State

INDIANA
At a Glance

Capital: Indianapolis

Major Industries: Metals, transportation equipment, electronics

Major Crops: Corn, soybeans, wheat, hay

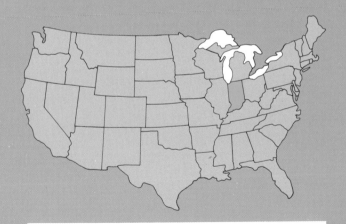

Size: 36,185 square miles (38th largest)
Population: 5,661,800 (14th largest)

State Flag

State Flag

The Indiana state flag, designed by Paul Hadley of Mooresville, was adopted in 1917. The background is blue, and in the center is a torch symbolizing freedom and knowledge. Around the flaming torch are seventeen stars in gold. On the handle of the torch is the eighteenth star. Above the flame is a nineteenth star, larger than the others, symbolizing Indiana's place as the nineteenth state. Above that is the word *Indiana*.

Indiana's racing tradition moves from the speedway to the water at the Regatta and Governor's Cup Race in Madison.

State Capital

Before statehood, the Indiana Territory had its capital in Vincennes (1800-13), and Corydon (1813-16). When Indiana became a state, Corydon remained the capital from 1816 to 1824. Indianapolis was named the capital in 1824. The first statehouse was built in 1835, but proved to be too small. The present capitol building, designed by Edwin May, was begun in 1878 and completed in 1888 at a cost of about $2 million. Built of Indiana limestone, it is four stories high and is topped by a golden dome, which reaches a height of 234 feet.

State Motto

The Crossroads of America

In 1937, the legislature created this motto. At the time, the center of the United States was in Indiana, and many north-south and east-west roads crossed in the state.

State Name and Nicknames

Indiana was named by the United States Congress when it created the Indiana Territory in 1800. The name simply means "Land of the Indians."

Officially, the nickname of Indiana is the *Crossroads of America,* as designated by the state legislature. But unofficially, it is most commonly referred to as the *Hoosier State.* No one seems to know the exact origin of the word "Hoosier," but there are several theories. Some say that a contractor, Samuel Hoosier, working on the Ohio Falls Canal at Louisville, Kentucky in 1826, gave employment preference to men living on the Indiana side of the Ohio River. These men became "Hoosier's Men." Others maintain that it stems from the early pioneers, who called out "Who's yare?" instead of "Who's there?" Still another explanation is that the word is a corruption of "husher," a word given to the early riverboat workers, who could hush anyone with brute force.

State Flower

The first state flower was adopted in 1913. From then on the state legislature kept changing its mind. At various times, the state flower was the carnation (family *Caryophyllus*), the flower of the tulip tree (*Liriodendron tulipfera*), and the zinnia (*Zinnia elegans*). In 1957, the peony (*Paeonia*) was adopted, even though the flower is not native to the state.

State Tree

Liriodendron tulipfera, the tulip tree, was named the Indiana state tree in 1931. Other names for the tree are yellow poplar, blue poplar, hickory poplar, basswood, cucumber tree, tulipwood, whitewood, white poplar, and old-wife's-shirt tree.

State Bird

The cardinal, *Richmondena Cardinalis cardinalis,* or redbird, was adopted as the state bird in 1933.

State Language

English has been the state

language of Indiana since 1984.

State Poem
In 1963, "Indiana," by Arthur Franklin Mapes, was named the state poem.

State Stone
Limestone was designated the state stone in 1971.

State Song
Selected in 1913, "On the Banks of the Wabash, Far Away," by Paul Dresser, is the state song.

Population
The population of Indiana in 1992 was 5,661,800, making it the 14th most populous state. There are 157.8 persons per square mile.

Industries
The principal industries of Indiana are trade, agriculture, and services. The chief manufactured products are metals, transportation equipment, electrical and electronic equipment, non-electrical machinery, plastics, chemical products, and food products.

Agriculture
The chief crops of the state are corn, sorghum, oats, wheat, rye, soybeans, and hay. Indiana is also a livestock state; and there are estimated to be some 1.2 million cattle, 4.4 million hogs and pigs, 82,757 sheep, and 28 million chickens on its farms. Oak, tulip, beech, and sycamore trees are cut. Crushed stone, cement, gypsum, lime, sand, and gravel are important mineral resources. Commercial fishing earned $2.55 million in 1992.

The scenic beauty of the Ohio River is equalled by its great history. Exhibits at the Ohio River Museum cover the early days of navigation and the age of steamboat travel.

Government

The governor of Indiana is elected to a four-year term, as are the lieutenant governor, attorney general, secretary of state, auditor, treasurer, and superintendent of public instruction. All other elected state officers serve two-year terms. The state legislature, or general assembly, which meets annually, consists of a 50-member senate and a 100-member house of representatives. Legislators are elected from senatorial and house districts. Senators serve four-year terms, and representatives serve two-year terms. The most recent state constitution was adopted in 1851. In addition to its two U.S. senators, Indiana has ten representatives in the U.S. House of Representatives. The state has twelve votes in the electoral college.

Sports

Many sporting events on the collegiate and secondary school level are scheduled all over the state. Indiana has always been known as the premier basketball state, and the sport's popularity is referred to as "Hoosier Hysteria." For example, the state high school basketball tournament is not divided into classes; rather every high school in the state participates until a champion is crowned. Indeed, the first high school basketball championship game ever televised nationally was the 1989 Indiana final game.

On the collegiate level in basketball, Indiana University has won the NCAA national championship five times. In football, Purdue won the Rose bowl in 1967. The University of Notre Dame, a perennial football power, has made many post-season bowl appearances. On the

Basketball is the top sport in the state, and Notre Dame has produced many fine teams.

professional level, the Indianapolis Colts of the National Football League play in the Hoosier Dome, and the Indiana Pacers of the National Basketball Association play in Market Square Arena in Indianapolis.

Major Cities

Evansville (population 126,272). Founded in 1812 by Colonel Hugh McGary, it was sold to General Robert Evans in 1818, for whom it was renamed. It was incorporated as a town in 1819 and chartered as a city in 1847. Located on the north bank of the Ohio River, it has retained some of the atmosphere of the days when steamboats plied the waters of the river. It is the principal transportation, trade, and industrial center of southern Indiana and the producer of a wide array of manufactured goods.

Things to see in Evansville: Evansville Museum of Arts and Science, Reitz Home (1871), Wesselman Park, Angel Mounds State Historic Site, and Mesker Park Zoo.

Fort Wayne (population 172,971). Settled about 1690, Fort Wayne is located where the St. Joseph and St. Mary's rivers join to form the Maumee River. Originally the headquarters of the Miami Indians, here the French established a fort in 1690. Fort Wayne became a major stop on the first railroad between Chicago

Evansville's Old Vanderburgh County Courthouse, built in 1890, is now home to a theater group, a dance company, and art galleries.

and Pittsburgh in the 1850s, laying the foundation for the city's industrial development.

Things to see in Fort Wayne: Allen County-Fort Wayne Historical Society Museum, Louis A. Warren Lincoln Library and Museum, Fort Wayne Museum of Art, Historic Fort Wayne, Cathedral of the Immaculate Conception, Children's Zoo, Lakeside Rose Garden, and Foellinger-Freimann Botanical Conservatory.

Gary (population 116,646). Founded and incorporated in 1906 by the United States Steel Corporation, it was built on dunes and swampland and named for its chairman, Elbert H. Gary. Located on the southern tip of Lake Michigan in Northwestern Indiana, this site was chosen for its railroad and transport accessibility to the resources necessary for steelmaking.

Things to see in Gary: Indiana Dunes State Park and Dunes National Lakeshore.

Tippecanoe Place in South Bend is near the site of the Battle of Tippecanoe, where William Henry Harrison's men fought Tecumseh's Shawnee warriors.

Indianapolis (population 731,327). In 1820 the pastoral area of rolling woodlands at the crossing of the Fall Creek and White Water rivers was selected as the site for the state's future capital. The legislature first met in Indianapolis in 1825. In 1847 it was incorporated as a city and had a population of 8,000. Chosen because it was at the geographical center of the state, the city was laid out in the wheel pattern of Washington, D.C. By the beginning of this century, it had developed into a manufacturing center. A cosmopolitan city, it has become the amateur sports capital of the United States.

Things to see in Indianapolis: State Capitol (1878-88), War Memorials Plaza, City Market, Union Station, President Benjamin Harrison Memorial Home (1874), Historic Lockerbie Square, James Whitcomb Riley Home, Scottish Rite Cathedral, Crown Hill Cemetery, Indiana Convention Center/Hoosier Dome, National track and Field Hall of Fame, State Library and Historical Building, Indiana State Museum, Morris-Butler House (1864), Indianapolis Museum of Art, Krannert Pavilion, Lilly Pavilion of Decorative Arts, Clowes Pavilion, Children's Museum, Eiteljorg Museum of the American Indian and Western Art, Patrick Henry Sullivan Museum, Muncie Art Center, Indianapolis Motor Speedway and Hall of Fame Museum, Hook's Historical Drug Store and Pharmacy Museum, Garfield Park, and Indianapolis Zoo.

South Bend (population 105,511). Founded in 1823, the site was first visited by the explorers Father Marquette and Louis Jolliet between 1673 and 1675. But it was not until 1820 that a trading post was set up in the area. In 1823, Alexis Coquillard and Francis Comparet founded the town and began its industrial development. Today it is the industrial, cultural, and educational center of the north-central part of the state.

Things to see in South Bend:
Northern Indiana Historical Society Museum (1855), Council Oak Tree, Snite Museum of Art and O'Shaughnessy Hall Galleries, Church of the Sacred Heart (1871), Grotto of Our Lady of Lourdes, Century Center, Warner Gallery and Women's Art League gallery, The Studebaker National Museum, City Greenhouses and Conservatory, Rum Village, and East Race Waterway.

Places to Visit

The National Park Service maintains four areas in the state of Indiana: Lincoln Boyhood National Memorial, Indiana Dunes National Lakeshore, George Rogers Clark National Historical Park, and Hoosier National Forest. In addition, there are 41 state recreation areas.

Auburn: Auburn-Cord-Duesenberg Museum. Three huge showrooms contain more than 140 antique cars, many of them illustrating Indiana's automotive past.
Bloomington: Thomas Hart Benton murals. Huge murals by the great painter can be seen in the Indiana University Auditorium.
Columbus: Architectural Tours. More than 50 public and business buildings designed by many world-famous architects can be seen in this small city.
Connersville: Whitewater Valley Railroad. Round-trip excursions can be taken on an early-1900s steam train.
French Lick: House of Clocks Museum displaying a large collection of clocks, some of them dating back to the early 1800s.
Jeffersonville: Howard Steamboat Museum.
Lafayette: Fort Ouiatenon. Reconstructions of the 1717 fort and trading post depict the history of the Wabash Valley.
Martinsville: Midwest Phonograph Museum. More than 600 antique record players and other memorabilia are on display.
Noblesville: Conner Prairie Settlement. A reconstruction of a prairie settlement of 1836.
Peru: Circus Museum. A vast collection of circus costumes and memorabilia.

Richmond: Levi Coffin House. This Federal-style brick house, built in 1839, was the home of a Quaker abolitionist who helped 2,000 fugitive slaves get to Canada.
Rockville: Historic Billie Creek Village. This is a recreation of a turn-of-the-century village and working farmstead.
Terre Haute: Eugene V. Debs home. This restored house was the home of the founder of the American Railway Union.
Warsaw: International Palace of Sports Hall of Fame. Displays wax figures of outstanding sports personalities.
Wyandotte: Wyandotte Cave. This limestone cavern is one of the world's largest.

Wyandotte Cave.

Events

There are many events and organizations that schedule activities of various kinds in the state of Indiana. Here are some of them:

Sports: Auto racing at International Dragway (Albany); Little 500 (Anderson); harness races and Free Fair (Anderson); Little 500 Bicycle Race (Bloomington); Whitewater Canoe Race (Connersville); Sugar Creek Canoe Race (Crawfordsville); GTE/US Men's Open Hardcourt Championships (Indianapolis); Indianapolis 500 Auto Race (Indianapolis); Regatta and Governor's Cup Race (Madison); Sprint Car races at Terre Haute Action Track (Terre Haute).

Arts and Crafts: Antique car and auto show (Aurora); Centerville Quilt Show (Centerville); Greentown Glass Festival (Kokomo); Midsummer Arts Festival (Lafayette).

Music: Indiana University Opera Theater (Bloomington); Ohio River Arts Festival (Evansville); Evansville Philharmonic (Evansville); Fort Wayne Philharmonic (Fort Wayne); Indianapolis Symphony (Indianapolis); Indianapolis Opera (Indianapolis); Footlight Musicals (Indianapolis); Starlight Musicals (Indianapolis); Fiddlers' Gathering (Lafayette); Marion Philharmonic (Marion); Lakefront Music Fest (Michigan City); South Bend Symphony (South Bend); Firefly Festival of the Performing Arts (South Bend).

Entertainment: Gaslight Festival (Anderson); Victorian Christmas (Aurora); Monroe County Fair (Bloomington); Madrigal Feasts (Bloomington); Harrison County Fair (Corydon); Germania Maennerchor Volkfest (Evansville); Germanfest (Fort Wayne); Three Rivers Festival (Fort Wayne); Johnny Appleseed Festival (Fort Wayne); Orange County Pumpkin Festival (French Lick); August Fest (Hammond); International Culture Festival (Hammond); Huntington County Heritage Days (Huntington); "500" Festival (Indianapolis); Indiana State Fair (Indianapolis); Steamboat Days Festival (Jeffersonville); Antique Steam Show (Lafayette); La Porte County Fair (La Porte); Iron Horse Festival (Logansport); Marion Easter Pageant (Marion); Michigan City Summer Festival (Michigan City); Summerfest

The Indianapolis 500 is the largest one-day sporting event in the world; it draws about 400,000 spectators every year.

(Mishawaka); Delaware County Fair (Muncie); Wine and Craft Festival (Nashville); Circus City Festival (Peru); Rose Festival (Richmond); Pioneer Day Festival (Richmond); Round Barn Festival (Rochester); Trail of Courage Rendezvous (Rochester); Civil War Days (Rockville); Parke County covered Bridge Festival (Rockville); "Thinking of Christmas" (Rockville); Rush County Fair (Rushville); Blue River Valley Pioneer Fair (Shelbyville); Maple Syrup Festival (South Bend); Ethnic Festival (South Bend); Sweet Sorghum Celebration (South Bend); Maple Sugarin' Days (Terre Haute); Wabash Valley Festival (Terre Haute); Spirit of Vincennes Rendezvous (Vincennes); Civil War Re-Enactment (Warsaw).

The Circus City Festival in Peru displays circus costumes and paraphernalia. Peru served as winter quarters for several traveling circuses.

Lincoln Boyhood National Memorial.

Tours: Gaslight Christmas (Anderson); Christmas Candlelight Tour (Crawfordsville); Candlelight Nights Tour (Madison); Log Cabin Tour (Nashville).

Theater: Shawnee Theater (Bloomfield); Embassy Theatre (Fort Wayne); Foellinger Theatre (Fort Wayne); Hilton U. Brown Theatre (Indianapolis); Indianapolis Civic Theater (Indianapolis); Indiana Repertory Theater (Indianapolis); "Young Abe Lincoln" (Lincoln Boyhood National Memorial); Marion Civic Theatre (Marion); Dunes Summer Theater (Michigan City); Canterbury Summer Theater (Michigan City); Brown County Playhouse (Nashville).

The Land and the Climate

Indiana is bounded on the west by Illinois, on the north by Michigan and Lake Michigan, on the east by Ohio, and on the south by Kentucky. There are three main land regions in the state. From north to south, they are the Great Lakes Plains, the Till Plains, and the Southern Hills and Lowlands.

The Great Lakes Plains, sometimes called the Northern Lake and Moraine Region, are part of a larger area of fertile lowlands along the shoreline of the Great Lakes. Here sand dunes rim Lake Michigan, with farmlands of dark, rich soil to the south. The farmers of the region raise beef cattle, soybeans, potatoes, poultry, vegetables, and corn.

The Till Plains of central Indiana, composed of soil and other materials (till) deposited during the Ice Age, are part of the great Midwestern Corn Belt. Low hills dot the region, which includes, in Wayne county, the highest point in the state—1,257 feet above sea level. The Till Plains produce fruit, corn, soybeans, and vegetables. Livestock graze on the region's pastures.

Farming is important to Indiana's economy. The state's rich soil and moderate climate make it one of the nation's leading agricultural areas.

Northeastern Indiana is part of the Great Lakes Plains, which consist of fertile lowlands with dark, rich soil. Major lakes in this region include Lakes Wawasee and Manitou and Turkey Lake.

The Southern Hills and Lowlands are the hilliest part of Indiana. This area was untouched by the ancient glaciers. It is a land of limestone caves and steep hills, called knobs. Here are limestone quarries, coal mines, and petroleum wells. Crops grown here include hay, tobacco, wheat, barley, corn, and fruit. Hogs, poultry, and beef and dairy cattle are also raised in the area.

Indiana's most important rivers include the Wabash, the White, the Tippecanoe, the St. Joseph, and the Salamonie. The state has about 36 sizable lakes, of which Lake Wawasee, in the northeast, is the largest. Manitou, Maxinkuckee, and Turkey Lakes are also in northeastern Indiana.

The climate of Indiana is marked by sharply defined seasons and sometimes sudden weather changes. Rainfall, spread throughout the year, averages about 40 inches. Winter temperatures range from about 29 degrees Fahrenheit in the north to 35 degrees F. in the south, although zero-degree weather and heavy snowfalls are not uncommon. Summer averages range from 73 to 86 degrees F. and temperatures over 100 degrees F. have been recorded. Humidity is often high.

Southern Indiana is the hilliest part of the state. This mineral-rich area has coal mines, oil wells, and limestone caves.

The History

About 3,000 years ago, the people who lived in what would become Indiana began to cultivate tobacco and food plants, including sunflower, gourds, squash, and corn. They made pottery and objects carved from sandstone, and constructed huge mounds of earth in which they buried their dead. We know them as the Adena people. Later groups such as the Hopewell built even larger earth mounds that served as fortified villages and ritual areas. Some of these can still be seen. But by the time the Europeans arrived in the 17th century, there were only a few hundred Indians in the territory, primarily members of the Miami tribe, some of whom remain to this day.

During the 1700s and 1800s, Indians from the east came into the area as their lands were taken over by white settlers. These included the Delaware, Mahican, Munsee, and Shawnee. Still others came from the northern Great Lakes region. Among them were the Huron, Kickapoo, Piankashaw, Potawatomi, and Wea tribes. The Potawatomi were the last to enter and the last to leave Indiana; most of them were induced to sell their land to the U.S. government, and others were evicted by military force in 1838. But some Potawatomi remain near South Bend.

The first Europeans to visit the region were probably the Jesuit missionary Jacques Marquette and his companion, Louis Joliet, who traveled through northern Indiana and preached to the Indians in 1673. In 1679 came the French explorer Robert Cavelier, known as La Salle. He started out from French Canada in search of a water route to the Pacific Ocean and traveled down the St. Joseph and Kankakee Rivers. La Salle returned to the region in 1680, reinforcing the French claim to Indiana. French fur traders from Canada came to offer beads, blankets, knives, and whiskey to the Indians in exchange for animal furs. They established trading posts at Miami, near

Fort Wayne was originally the site of a trading post built by the French who protected their trade route between Montreal, Canada and New Orleans, Louisiana, with a series of stockades during the 1700s. The first European settlements grew up along this route.

present-day Fort Wayne, and at Ouiatenon, where Lafayette is today. About 1731 the first permanent white settlement in Indiana was established by the French at Vincennes; a fort was built there two years later.

British fur traders also came into Indiana and clashed with the French. The French claimed the territory because of La Salle's explorations, and the British claimed it as an extension of their Atlantic Seaboard colonies. When the French and Indian Wars broke out, the British finally defeated the French, who gave up their claim to Indiana and other North American holdings in 1763. The French left few marks on the land except for the names of such cities as Vincennes, Terre Haute, and La Porte.

During the Revolutionary War, British troops began to occupy the region. They moved into Vincennes in 1777 and took control of Fort Sackville. In 1778 the American leader George Rogers Clark captured the fort with Virginia frontiersmen and claimed southern Indiana for the state of Virginia. The British recaptured the outpost, but Clark seized it again in 1779. However, faraway Virginia was unable to control the region, and Indiana became public domain in 1784. It was made part of the Northwest Territory in 1787.

Fort Vincennes guarded the French settlement of Vincennes, founded about 1731. It was Indiana's first European settlement.

Settlers from the east began to filter in after the Revolution ended in 1783, traveling down the Ohio River (now Indiana's southern boundary) and across Kentucky in what would become a steady stream. Many were former soldiers who held land grants from the government that it had issued instead of back pay. They cleared fields, built settlements, and lived in log cabins. One pioneer couple named Lincoln had come from Kentucky with their young son, Abraham. Soon after they arrived, the mother, Nancy Hanks Lincoln, died, and the boy Abraham helped his father bury her in the forest. It was during the pioneer era that Indiana got its future nickname of the Hoosier State, perhaps from the regional greeting to visitors, "Who's here?"

The Miami Indians, under the leadership of Chief Little Turtle, resisted white encroachments on their land. Aided by the British, Little Turtle and his forces successfully fought off attacks by U.S. government troops in 1790 and 1791. However, in 1794 federal troops under General Anthony Wayne defeated the Miami and allied tribes in the Battle of Fallen Timbers, near present-day Toledo, Ohio.

The Indiana Territory, created in 1800, included what is now Indiana, Illinois, Wisconsin, and parts of Michigan and Minnesota. President John Adams appointed General William Henry Harrison, who was later to be president himself, the territorial governor, with his capital at Vincennes.

Continuing pressure on the Indians by the federal government in Washington and by white settlers led the great Shawnee chief Tecumseh to form a Confederation of Indian Nations that would extend from the Great Lakes to the Gulf of Mexico. While Tecumseh was away gathering support in the south in 1811, Harrison defeated the Indians in the Battle of Tippecanoe, near present-day Lafayette. This dealt a fatal blow to the Indian organization.

The Indians then joined British forces against the Americans in the War of 1812, but federal troops and militia burned their towns and granaries. The Indians stood with the British in a last furious attempt to defend their land, but Tecumseh's death in the Battle of the

William Henry Harrison became the first governor of the Indiana Territory when it was created in 1800, with Vincennes as its capital. Conflict with the Indians over land rights culminated in the 1811 Battle of Tippecanoe, in which Harrison defeated the confederation led by Shawnee chief Tecumseh.

Thames River in Canada two years later marked the end of their resistance in Indiana. Corydon became the new capital of the Indiana Territory in 1813. Settlers began to pour in, including thousands of immigrants from Europe. Among them were the Swiss, who moved into the forests to do woodworking and make furniture. They named Switzerland County and the river settlement of Tell City. Germans helped develop Terre Haute and Indianapolis, becoming bankers, brewers, and civic leaders.

Indiana joined the Union in 1816 as the 19th state, and in 1821 Indianapolis was named the new state capital. Railroads began pushing into the state in the 1850s and the economy expanded. Farmers had new markets for their crops, and industries for their products. The Studebaker brothers opened their blacksmith and wagon shop in South Bend in 1852, and it was soon the largest

wagon-making factory in the country (later it became an important automobile manufacturer). Richard Gatling had invented the first practical machine gun in Indianapolis in 1862. During the 1860s James Oliver improved the steel plow invented by John Deere to cut through the tough prairie land.

There was only one battle in Indiana during the Civil War—the Battle of Corydon. John Hunt Morgan, a Confederate cavalry general, led Morgan's Raiders up from Kentucky to raid the former state capital. Then they rode on to Ohio.

Throughout the last half of the 19th century, the character of Indiana changed slowly from rural-agricultural to highly industrialized. One of the first gasoline pumps in the United States was manufactured at Fort Wayne in 1885. Natural gas was discovered near Portland the following year. In 1889 the Standard Oil Company built one of the world's largest oil refineries in the little village of Whiting. In 1894 Elwood Haynes of Kokomo designed one of the first successful gasoline-powered automobiles.

Oliver P. Morton was governor of Indiana during the Civil War era, when the state endured a grave political and financial crisis.

The Kepler House still stands in New Harmony, the experimental community that established the first coeducational school in the United States in 1825.

In 1906 the United States Steel Corporation selected a tract of sand dunes on the south shore of Lake Michigan as the site of a new steel-making city, to be called Gary. The city became the core of a vast industrial complex devoted to steel, iron, and chemicals, stretching 45 miles along the shore of the lake in the great Calumet Region. The first 500-mile race was held at the Indianapolis Motor Speedway in 1911, attesting to Indiana's confidence in the future of the automobile.

Six years later, the United States entered World War I, in which more than 130,000 Indiana men served. Although agriculture remained important to the state's economy after the war, the auto-mobile and metal-products industries continued to expand. The steelworkers of Gary, located in one of the greatest steel-producing areas in the world, led the steel strike of 1919-20, in which federal troops occupied the city for three months. To diversify the econ-omy, the city encouraged the production of steel-related goods, as well as chemicals, plastics, and petroleum. These thriving indus-tries, which attracted many European immigrants in the early 20th century, made a vital contribution to the nation's economic growth and welfare.

More than 340,000 men and women from Indiana served in the armed forces during World War II, when the state's steel and fuel were important to the war effort. In the second half of the 20th century, Indiana's location at the crossroads of the nation has made it one of the most typically American states in the Union. It has grown increasingly since the 1920s to become an urban and indus-trial society, with booming cities such as Gary attracting many southern blacks and Latin Americans. Since there is no dominant city, the distribution of the population between numerous cities has enabled Indiana to preserve its rural influence. Against the still visible background of Indian history and the determined pioneer struggle for survival, Indiana stands out as a region that has come of age.

The University of Notre Dame, in South Bend, is one of the leading Roman Catholic universities in the country.

The world-famous "Indy 500" automobile race is held each year at the Indianapolis Motor Speedway. The 500-mile race is part of an annual event that attracts thousands of visitors during the Memorial Day weekend.

Education

Indiana was the first state in the nation to provide in its constitution for a state-wide system of free public education—in 1816. In 1825 the experimental community of New Harmony established the first coeducational school in the United States. The first public library in the state was opened in 1807 in Vincennes. Indiana University, the first institution of higher education, opened in 1820, just four years after statehood. Many others followed. By the beginning of the Civil War in 1861, there were 15 colleges and universities.

The People

More than 68 percent of Hoosiers live in metropolitan areas including Indianapolis, Fort Wayne, and Evansville, and 98 percent of them were born in the United States. The biggest single religious group in the state consists of Roman Catholics, although the Protestant churches combined have a larger membership. Sizable Protestant denominations include the Baptists, Lutherans, Methodists, Presbyterians, and members of the Disciples of Christ. Historically, the majority of foreign-born citizens came from Germany; other non-native groups include British, Canadians, Czechs, Hungarians, Italians, and Poles.

Astronaut Virgil Ivan "Gus" Grissom, a native of Mitchell, Indiana, was the first American to make two trips into space.

Songwriter Cole Porter, born in Peru, Indiana, provided words and music for more than 30 Broadway and Hollywood hits, including *Kiss Me Kate* and *Anything Goes*.

Famous People

Many famous people were born in the state of Indiana. Here are a few:

Philip W. Anderson b. 1923, Indianapolis. Nobel Prize-winning physicist

Anne Baxter 1923-1985, Michigan City. Academy Award-winning actress: *The Razor's Edge, All About Eve*

Charles A. Beard 1874-1948, near Knightstown. Historian

Larry Bird b. 1956, French Lick. Basketball player

Bill Blass b. 1922, Fort Wayne. Fashion designer

Frank Borman b. 1928, Gary. Astronaut

Three Finger Brown 1876-1948, Nyesville. Hall of Fame pitcher

Ambrose Burnside 1824-1881, Liberty. Union Army general

Max Carey 1890-1976, Terre Haute. Hall of Fame baseball player

Hoagy Carmichael 1899-1981, Bloomington. Song composer

Oscar Charleston 1896-1954, Indianapolis. Hall of Fame baseball player

Eddie Condon 1905-1973, Goodland. Jazz guitarist

Adelle Davis 1904-1974, Lizton. Nutritionist

James Dean 1931-1955, Marion. Film actor: *Rebel Without a Cause, Giant*

Eugene Debs 1855-1926, Terre Haute. Union leader

Lloyd C. Douglas 1877-1951, Columbia City. Novelist: *Magnificent Obsession, The Robe*

Theodore Dreiser 1871-1945, Terre Haute. Novelist: *Sister Carrie, An American Tragedy*

Ray Ewry 1873-1937, Lafayette. Track and field athlete who won eight Olympic medals

Ford Frick 1894-1978, near Wawaka. Hall of Fame baseball executive

Bernard F. Gimbel 1885-1966, Vincennes. Department store executive

Bob Griese b. 1945, Evansville. Hall of Fame football quarterback

Gus Grissom 1926-1967, Mitchell. Astronaut

Roy Halston 1932-1990, Evansville. Fashion designer

Richard G. Hatcher b.1933, Michigan City. First black mayor of Gary

Howard Hawks 1896-1977, Goshen. Movie director: *To Have and Have Not, Rio Bravo*

Jimmy Hoffa 1913-1975, Brazil. Teamsters union president

Michael Jackson b. 1958, Gary. Pop singer

J.J. Johnson b. 1924, Indianapolis. Jazz trombonist

Alex Karras b. 1935, Gary. Football player, actor

David Letterman b. 1947, Indianapolis. Television

talk show host

Eli Lilly 1885-1977, Indianapolis. Drug manufacturer and philanthropist

Carole Lombard 1908-1942, Fort Wayne. Film actress: *Nothing Sacred, To Be or Not to Be*

Wes Montgomery 1925-1968, Indianapolis. Jazz guitarist

Jane Pauley b. 1950, Indianapolis. TV anchorwoman

Cole Porter 1893-1964, Peru. Composer of popular songs and musicals

Ernie Pyle 1900-1945, Dana. Pulitzer Prize-winning war correspondent

J. Danforth "Dan" Quayle b. 1947, Indianapolis. U.S. Vice-president 1988-92

James Whitcomb Riley 1849-1916, Greenfield. Poet: *The Old Swimmin' Hole and 'Leven More Poems, Afterwhiles*

Paul Samuelson b. 1915, Gary. Nobel Prize-winning economist

Rex Stout 1886-1975, Noblesville. Mystery writer and creator of Nero Wolfe: *Black Orchids, The Doorbell Rang*

Booth Tarkington 1869-1946, Indianapolis. Two-time Pulitzer Prize-winning novelist: *The Magnificent Ambersons, Alice Adams*

Twyla Tharp b. 1941, Portland. Dancer and choreographer

Kurt Thomas b. 1956, Terre Haute. Olympic Gold

Wilbur Wright and his brother Orville were pioneers of air travel. In 1903, they became the first to build and fly an engine-powered airplane.

Medal-winning gymnast

Harold Urey 1893-1981, Walkerton. Nobel Prize-winning chemist

Kurt Vonnegut b. 1922, Indianapolis. Novelist: *Slaughterhouse Five, Slapstick*

Lew Wallace 1827-1905, Brookville. Novelist: *Ben Hur*

Jessamyn West 1902-1984, near North Vernon. Novelist: *The Friendly Persuasion, A Matter of Time*

Wendell Wilkie 1892-1944, Elwood. Leader of the fight against isolationism during World War I

Robert Wise b. 1914, Winchester. Two-time Academy Award-winning movie director: *West Side Story, The Sound of Music*

John Wooden b. 1910, Martinsville. Named to the Basketball Hall of Fame both as a player and a coach

Wilbur Wright 1867-1912, near Millville. Co-designer of the first airplane

Colleges and Universities

There are many colleges and universities in Indiana. Here are the most prominent, with their locations, dates of founding, and enrollments.

Anderson College, Anderson, 1917, 2,249

Ball State University, Muncie, 1918, 20,333

Butler University, Indianapolis, 1855, 3,825

DePauw University, Greencastle, 1837, 2,058

Earlham College, Richmond, 1847, 1,106

Hanover College, Hanover, 1827, 1,071

Fall foliage at Indiana University at Bloomington, one of many fine universities in the state.

Indiana Institute of Technology, Fort Wayne, 1930, 1,150

Indiana State University, Terre Haute, 1865, 12,271

Indiana University, at Kokomo, 1945, 3,522; *at South Bend,* 1922, 7,800; *at Bloomington,* 1820, 36,076; *at Richmond,* 1971, 2,411; *at Gary,* 1959, 5,963; *at New Albany,* 1941, 5,942.

Indiana University-Purdue University at Fort Wayne, 1917, 12,090; *at Indianapolis,* 1969, 28,345

Indiana Wesleyan University, Marion, 1920, 3,450

Manchester College, North Manchester, 1889, 1,080

Marian College, Indianapolis, 1851, 1,288

Purdue University, West Lafayette, 1869, 36,163; *Calumet,* at Hammond, 1951, 8,285; *North Central,* at Westville, 1967, 3,588

Rose-Hulman Institute of Technology, Terre Haute, 1874, 1,420

Saint Joseph's College, Rensselaer, 1889, 1,000

Saint Mary-of-the-Woods College, Saint Mary-of-the-Woods, 1840, 1,258

Saint Mary's College, Notre Dame, 1844, 1,576

Taylor University, Upland, 1846, 1,817

University of Notre Dame, Notre Dame, 1842, 10,000

University of Southern Indiana, Evansville, 1965, 7,430

Valparaiso University, Valparaiso, 1859, 3,757

Where To Get More Information

Indiana Department of Commerce
Tourism Development Division
One North Capitol Street
Suite 700
Indianapolis, IN 46204
Or call 1-800-289-6646

Michigan

The Great Seal of Michigan was designed in 1835 and adopted in 1911. It is circular, and on it is a shield supported by an elk and a moose. On the shield is a man standing on a peninsula with his right hand raised and a rifle in his left. The sun is shining on him. On the top of the shield is the word *Tuebor*, which means "I will defend" in Latin. Under the seal is the state motto. Above the shield is an eagle holding an olive branch and three arrows. Around the seal is written "The Great Seal of the State of Michigan" and "A.D. MDCCCXXXV" — the date 1835 in Roman numerals — the year of the design of the seal and also the year that the first constitution of the state was framed.

MICHIGAN

At a Glance

Capital: Lansing

Major Crops: Corn, winter wheat, soybeans, oats, fruit
Major Industries: Automobiles, machine tools, food processing

State Flag

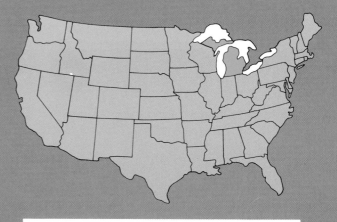

Size: 58,527 (23rd largest)
Population: 9,436,628 (8th largest)

N
△

ONTARIO

★ State Capital
● Cities or towns
■ OF SPECIAL INTEREST

Keweenaw Bay

LAKE SUPERIOR

Whitefish Bay

SAULT SAINTE MARIE

OTTAWA
NATIONAL
FOREST

HIAWATHA
NATIONAL
FOREST

WISCONSIN

HIAWATHA
NATIONAL
FOREST

Green Bay

■ MACKINAW CITY

LAKE HURON

HURON
NATIONAL
FOREST

MICHIGAN

Saginaw Bay

MANISTEE
NATIONAL
FOREST

WISCONSIN

Bay City ●

● Saginaw

LAKE
MICHIGAN

Muskegon ●

Grand Rapids ●

Flint ●

Port Huron ●

● Wyoming

★ **Lansing**

Lake Saint Clair

● Holland

Pontiac ●

Battle Creek

Detroit

ILLINOIS

Kalamazoo ●

Jackson ●

■ DEARBORN

Ann Arbor ●

● Adrian

Monroe ●

LAKE ERIE

INDIANA   OHIO

State Flower:
Apple Blossom

State Bird: Robin

0   20   60   100 Miles
0   20   60   100   150 Kilometres

33

State Flag

The state flag of Michigan was adopted in 1911. It is blue, and in the center is the state seal.

State Motto

Si Quaeris Peninsulam Amoenam Circumspice
The translation of this Latin motto is "If You Seek a Pleasant Peninsula, Look About You."

State Pledge of Allegiance

Adopted in 1972, the state pledge of allegiance reads: "I pledge allegiance to the flag of Michigan, and to the state for which it stands, two beautiful peninsulas united by a bridge of steel, where equal opportunity and justice to all is our ideal."

The lighthouse at Manistee, a Lake Michigan village that sits at the mouth of the Little Manistee River.

State Capital

Detroit was the capital of Michigan from 1835 to 1847, when the capital was moved to Ingham Township. A new capital city was built in what had been woods. First called Michigan, the town was shortly renamed Lansing.

State Name and Nicknames

European explorers named Lake Michigan in 1672 after a clearing on the west side of the lower peninsula. In Ojibwa, the word for clearing is "majigan," and the state took the name of the lake.

Even though few Michiganders have ever seen the animal, the state is called the *Wolverine State* since wolverines used to roam the territory. Because of the Great Lakes that surround the state, it is also called the *Great Lakes State* and the *Lady of the Lake*. Finally, because of its prominence in the automotive industry, it is called the *Auto State*.

State Flower

The blossom of the apple tree, *Pyrus coronaria*, was named the state flower in 1897.

State Tree

Pinus strobus, the white pine, was adopted as the state tree in 1955. It is also called eastern white pine, northern white pine, soft pine, Weymouth pine, and spruce pine.

State Bird

In 1931, the robin, *Turdus migratorius*, was named the state bird.

State Fish

The trout, family *Salmonidae*, was adopted as the state fish in 1966.

State Gem

Named in 1973, the chlorastrolite, or greenstone, is the state gem.

State Stone

The Petoskey stone was adopted as state stone in 1966.

State Song

"Michigan, My Michigan," with words by Douglas Malloch and music by W. Otto Meissner, is the unofficial state song of Michigan.

Population

The population of Michigan in 1992 was 9,436,628, making it the eighth most populous state. There are 166.1 persons per square mile. About 80 percent of the people live in metropolitan areas. Approximately 96 percent of Michiganians were born in the United States. Most of those born in other countries came from Canada. Other foreign-born groups include Poles, Italians, English, Germans, Russians, Scots, Dutch, Fins, and Swedes. The largest religious group in the state is made up of Roman Catholics. Other important denominations include the Episcopal, Lutheran, Methodist, and Presbyterian.

Industries

The principal industries of Michigan are mining, agriculture, food processing, and fishing. The chief manufactured products are automobiles, machine tools, chemicals, cereals, metals and metal products, plastics, and furniture.

Agriculture

The chief crops of the state are corn, winter wheat, soybeans, dry beans, oats, hay, sugar beets, honey, asparagus, potatoes, sweet corn, apples, cherries, grapes, peaches, and blueberries. Michigan is also a livestock state, and there are estimated to be some 1.2 million cattle, 1.3 million hogs and pigs, 103,000 sheep, and 11.5 million poultry on its farms. Maple, oak, and aspen timber is cut. Iron ore, cement, crushed stone, sand, and gravel are important mineral resources. Commercial fishing earned $10.4 million in 1992.

A freighter sails past Isle Royale National Park in Lake Superior, the largest lake in the world.

Government

The governor of Michigan serves a term of four years, as do the lieutenant governor, secretary of state, and attorney general. The state legislature consists of a 38-member senate and a 110-member house of representatives. Senators serve four-year terms, and representatives serve two-year terms. The most recent state constitution was adopted in 1964. In addition to its two U.S. senators, Michigan has 16 representatives in the U.S. House of Representatives. The state has 18 votes in the electoral college.

Henry Ford Museum.

The seventh largest city in the nation, Detroit is the primary business, cultural, and educational center of Michigan.

Sports

Historically, Michigan has always been a sports-minded state. The first professional hockey team was formed in Houghton in 1903. In 1959, Hamtramck won the Little League World Series. On the college level, the NCAA basketball championship has been won by both Michigan State University (1979) and the University of Michigan (1989). In football, the University of Michigan and Michigan State have both won Rose Bowl games. The NCAA baseball championship has been won by the University of Michigan in 1953 and 1962. The NCAA national championship in hockey has been won by the University of Michigan, Michigan State University, and Michigan Tech. On the professional level, the Detroit Tigers of the American League play baseball at Tiger Stadium. The Detroit Pistons of the National Basketball Association play in the Palace of Auburn Hills in Auburn Hills. The Detroit Lions of the National Football League appear at the Pontiac Silverdome in Pontiac. The Detroit Red Wings of the National Hockey League play in the Joe Louis Sports Arena.

Major Cities

Ann Arbor (population 109,608). Settled in 1823 by John and Ann Allen from Virginia and Elisha and Ann Rumsey from New York. The settlement was named after

The Palace of Auburn Hills is home to the Detroit Pistons of the National Basketball Association.

the first names of the two wives. In 1824 it became the county seat and in 1851 was chartered as a city. It is located 36 miles west of Detroit on the Huron River and is the agricultural trading center of Michigan and a manufacturing center.

Places to visit in Ann Arbor:
The University of Michigan library and the surrounding hill regions and its many lakes and resorts.

Detroit (population 1,027,974). Founded in 1701 by Antoine de la Mothe Cadillac at *le place du détroit*—"the place of the strait"—it soon became an important French trading post. It was captured by the British in 1760 and was not turned over to the United States until 1796. The British recaptured the town during the War of 1812. Detroit was finally incorporated in 1815. At the turn of the century the automobile boom transformed the city, as many immigrants came to Detroit to seek jobs.

Five of the six major U.S. automobile manufacturers are headquartered here and one-fifth of automobiles made in the United States are manufactured in the Detroit area. In the late 1960s, Detroit was torn apart by race riots, as were many other American cities—43 lives were lost in Detroit race riots in 1967. Detroit's population dropped by 611,000 from 1950 to 1980, as many white Detroiters moved to the suburbs of the city.

The auto industry was hard hit by the recession of the early 1980s and many automobile plants were closed and workers were laid off. Detroit is also famous for the popular music produced by Motown Records.

Things to see in Detroit:
Mariners' Church (1848), Renaissance Center, People Mover, Washington Boulevard Trolley Car, Children's Museum, Detroit Institute of Arts, Detroit Historical Museum, Museum of African-American History, Detroit Public Library, Detroit Symphony Orchestra Hall, Detroit Science Center, Detroit Fire Department Historical Museum, Fisher Building, New Center One, Trinity Lutheran Church (1931), Historic Fort Wayne (1843-48), Detroit Zoo, Belle Isle, Whitcomb Conservatory, Safari-Trail Zoo, The Aquarium, Dossin Great Lakes Museum, Trappers Alley, Eastern Market (1892), and Boblo Island.

Flint (population 140,761). Settled as a fur-trading post in 1819, the city was originally called the Grand Traverse of Flint. It was chartered as Flint in 1855 and is located 58 miles northwest of Detroit on the Flint River in southeastern Michigan. One of the world's leading automobile manufacturing centers, it houses several

The Automobile in American Life is one exhibit at the Henry Ford Museum.

divisions of General Motors and the Buick Motor Company, the first automobile company to establish a plant here in 1904. In 1980 the General Motors Corporation employed three-fourths of the work force of Flint. Other manufactured products including automobile accessories, structural steel, chemicals, and cotton textiles

have helped Flint to diversify its economy in times of economic trouble.

Places to visit in Flint:
Robert T. Longway planetarium and the University of Michigan at Flint

Grand Rapids (population 189,126). Settled in 1826 by Louis Campau as a trading post, the city gets its name from the rapids in the Grand River, which flows through the town. It is a city of furniture manufacturing, parks, and education.
Things to see in Grand Rapids:
Gerald R. Ford Museum, Grand Rapids Art Museum, Public Museum of Grand Rapids, Grand Center, John Ball Zoo, Blandford Nature Center, *La Grande Vitesse*, a sculpture by Alexander Calder, and Fish Ladder.

Lansing (population 127,321). Settled in 1847, when the state capital moved here from Detroit, the city originally consisted of one log house and a sawmill. The city's industrial growth began when R. E. Olds opened his Oldsmobile plant, and today it is a community of government and commerce.

Things to see in Lansing: State Capitol, Michigan Historical Museum, Potter Park, Brenke River Sculpture and Fish Ladder, Carl G. Fenner Arboretum, Woldumar Nature Center, Impression 5 Science Museum, and R. E. Olds Transportation Museum.

Places To Visit

The National Park Service maintains seven areas in the state of Michigan: Isle Royale National Park, Sleeping Bear Dunes National Lakeshore, Pictured Rocks National Lakeshore, Hiawatha National Forest, Huron National Forest, Manistee National Forest, and Ottawa National Forest. In addition, there are 75 state recreation areas.

Albion: Gardner House Museum. Built in 1875, this is a restored Victorian home.

Battle Creek: Leila Arboretum. This 72-acre park contains native trees and shrubs, as well as the Kingman Museum of Natural History.

Bloomfield Hills: Cranbrook Gardens. Forty acres of formal and informal gardens can be explored on winding trails.

Cheboygan: The U.S. Coast Guard Cutter *Mackinaw*. One of the world's largest icebreakers, the *Mackinaw* can be toured when she is in port.

Copper Harbor: Delaware Mine Tour. This copper mine dates back to the 1850s.

Cranbrook Estate: The estate of George G. Booth and Ellen Scripps Booth has become a cultural and educational center. It includes an art museum, gardens, a natural history museum, and several nationally known schools.

Dearborn: Henry Ford Museum and Greenfield Village. The museum and the buildings in the village contain thousands of historical artifacts, as well as the homes of the Wright Brothers and Henry Ford.

Frankenmuth: Michigan's Own, Military and Space Museum containing memorabilia of Michigan war heroes and astronauts.

Gaylord: Call of the Wild Museum. More than 150 life-size North American wild animals are displayed in scenic exhibits.

Holland: Dutch Village. Here are buildings of Dutch architecture, canals, windmills, and tulips.

Iron Mountain: Iron Mountain Iron Mine. Tours are conducted through the mine.

Ishpeming: National Ski Hall of Fame and Ski Museum. This houses national trophies and displays of old ski equipment.

Kalamazoo: Kalamazoo Air Zoo. Restored aircraft from World War II, many in flying condition, are on exhibit.

Mackinac Island: Fort Mackinac. The construction of this fort began in 1780. Mackinac Bridge is one of the world's longest suspension bridges.

Mackinaw City: Colonial Michilimackinac. The fortified colonial village of the mid-18th century has been reconstructed on original foundations.

Muskegon: USS *Silversides*. A World War II submarine with an impressive war record is open to the public.

Port Austin: Pioneer Huron City. Eight preserved buildings built in the 19th-century.

Saginaw: Saginaw Rose Garden. This is a spectacular circular garden with 1,000 rosebushes.

Saugatuck: SS *Keewatin*. The restored turn-of-the-century steamship is now a marine museum.

Sault Ste. Marie: Soo Locks Boat Tours. Here one can take a trip through both the American and Canadian locks, Lake Superior, and Lake Huron.

Traverse City: Schooner *Madeline*. This is a full-scale replica of an 1850 Great Lakes vessel.

Putting on ice comes naturally to the people of Michigan, who host the Polar Ice Cap Golf Tournament every winter.

Events

There are many events and organizations that schedule activities of various kinds in the state of Michigan. Here are some of them:

Sports: MORC Sailboat Race (Alpena); Thimbleberry Blossom Festival (Copper Harbor); Grand Prix (Detroit); Polar Ice Cap Golf Tournament (Grand Haven); World's Championship Au Sable River Canoe Marathon (Grayling); Pine Mountain Ski Jumping Tournament (Iron Mountain); Upper Peninsula Championship Rodeo (Iron River); harness racing at Jackson Harness Raceway (Jackson); Michigan International Speedway (Jackson); White Pine Stampede (Mancelona); Pictured Rocks Road Race (Munising); Great Lakes International Sled Dog Race (Muskegon); Eagle Run Cross-Country Ski Race (Oscoda); Blue Water Festival/Mackinac Race (Port Huron); Tri-State Regatta (St. Joseph); Hobie Regatta (South Haven); Indian Summer Triathlon (Tawas City); Governor's Cup Hydroplane Races (Ypsilanti).

Arts and Crafts: Street Art Fair (Ann Arbor); Labor Day Arts Fair (Big Rapids); Waterfront Art Fair (Charlevoix); East Lansing Art Festival (East Lansing);

Kalamazoo County Flowerfest (Kalamazoo); Downtown Arts Festival (Lansing); Lilac Festival (Mackinac Island); Women's Club Antique Show (Mackinaw City); Art on the Rocks (Marquette); Arts Dockside (St. Ignace); Lake Bluff Art Fair (St. Joseph); Tawas Bay Waterfront Art Show (Tawas City).

Music: Ann Arbor Summer Festival (Ann Arbor); Cheboygan Opera House (Cheboygan); Tibbits Opera House (Coldwater); Michigan Opera Theatre (Detroit); Detroit Symphony (Detroit); Montreux Detroit Jazz Festival (Detroit); Flint Symphony (Flint); Music and Arts Festival (Grand Marais); Grand Rapids Symphony (Grand Rapids); National Music Camp (Interlochen); Kalamazoo Symphony (Kalamazoo); Lansing Symphony (Lansing); Hiawatha Music Co-op (Marquette); Matrix: Midland Festival (Midland); Great Lumbertown Music Festival (Muskegon); Meadow Brook Music Festival (Rochester); Saginaw Symphony (Saginaw); Frog Island Jazz Festival (Ypsilanti).

Entertainment: Highland Festival and Games (Alma); Alpena County Fair (Alpena); Cereal City Festival (Battle Creek); St. Stanislaus Polish

Festival (Bay City); Mayfest Festival (Bridgman); Apple Festival (Charlevoix); Northern Michigan Fair (Cheboygan); Winter Tip-Up Carnival (Coldwater); Muzzle Loaders Festival (Dearborn); Autumn Harvest Festival (Dearborn); International Auto Show (Detroit); International Freedom Festival (Detroit); Michigan State Fair (Detroit); Santa Claus Parade (Detroit); Riverfront Festivals (Detroit); Harbor Days (Elk Rapids); Upper Peninsula State Fair (Escanaba); Bavarian Festival (Frankenmuth); Winterfest (Gaylord); Alpenfest (Gaylord); Otsego County Fair (Gaylord); Venetian Boat Parade (Grand Haven); Milltown Festival (Grayling); Mushroom Festival (Harrison); Tulip Time Festival (Holland); Dickens Christmas (Holly); Winter Carnival (Houghton); Tip-Up-Town USA Ice Festival (Houghton Lake); Water Show (Iron Mountain); VJ Day (Iron River); Iron County Fair (Iron River); Rose Festival (Jackson); Civil War Muster and Battle Re-enactment (Jackson); Jackson County Fair (Jackson); Maple Sugaring Weekend (Kalamazoo); Michigan International Air Show (Kalamazoo); Wine and Harvest Festival (Kalamazoo); Festival of the Pines (Lake City); Riverfest (Lansing); Colonial

Michilimackinac Pageant (Mackinaw City); Voyageur's Rendezvous (Mackinaw City); Polish Heritage Festival (Manistee); International Food Festival (Marquette); Waterfront Festival (Menominee); Monroe County Fair (Monroe); Old French Town Days (Monroe); Four Flags Area Apple Festival (Niles); Onekama Days (Onekama); Indian Powwow (Petoskey); Emmet County Fair (Petoskey); Island City Festival (Plainwell); Ice Sculpture Spectacular (Plymouth); Feast of the Ste. Claire (Port Huron); Mitas Polka Fest (Saginaw); Antique Car Show (St. Ignace); Mint Festival (St. Johns); Blossomtime Festival (St. Joseph); Harbor Days (Saugatuck); National Blueberry Festival (South Haven); MarinerFest (Tawas City); Cherry Festival (Traverse City).

Tours: Historic Home Tour (Marshall); Wurtsmith Air Force Base Tours (Oscoda); Historic Home Tours (Owosso).

Theater: Calumet Theater (Calumet); Tibbits Professional Summer Theatre Series (Coldwater); The Theater Company-University of Detroit (Detroit); Community Circle Theater (Grand Rapids); Kalamazoo Civic Players (Kalamazoo); Ramsdell Theater (Manistee); Midland Center for

The Fox Theater is a beautifully renovated auditorium in Detroit where touring productions are performed.

the Arts (Midland); Meadow Brook Theatre (Rochester); Cherry County Playhouse (Traverse City).

The Land and the Climate

The Lower Peninsula of Michigan is bordered on the west by Lake Michigan; on the north by Lakes Michigan and Huron; on the east by Lakes Huron and Erie and the Canadian province of Ontario; and on the south by Indiana and Ohio. The Upper Peninsula is bounded on the west and north by Lake Superior, on the east by Ontario, and on the south by Wisconsin and Lakes Michigan and Huron. There are two main land regions in the state: the Superior Upland and the Great Lakes Plains.

Most of Michigan is surrounded by four of the five Great Lakes. The state's coastline includes protected bays and capes that jut into Lakes Michigan, Superior, Huron, and Erie.

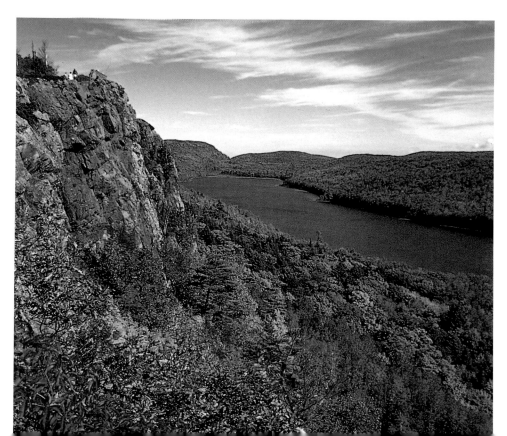

All of Michigan's rivers flow into the Great Lakes. The state's largest rivers are located in the Lower Peninsula.

Most of Michigan's sandy beaches are along the coast of the Lower Peninsula. Miles of shoreline provide ample opportunities for recreation and contribute to the state's economy.

The Superior Upland covers the western half of the Upper Peninsula and is part of a larger land area shared with Wisconsin and Minnesota. Most of the Upland consists of a rugged plateau that ranges from 600 to 2,000 feet above sea level. The Porcupine Mountains are here, most of them covered with forests. Iron and copper are mined in the region, and forestry and forest products are other chief industries.

The Great Lakes Plains cover the rest of the state—the eastern Upper Peninsula and all of the Lower Peninsula. This is part of a region that stretches along the Great Lakes from Wisconsin to Ohio. Much of the land is flat, but hills occur in some parts of it. The shores of Lake Michigan have many high bluffs and sand dunes. In the Upper Peninsula, forest products and stone quarrying are major industries. The Lower Peninsula, where most of the farming is done, has richer soil and a longer growing season. Wheat, vegetables, fruit, potatoes, corn, poultry, and beef and dairy cattle are raised here. The region also has oil and natural gas wells.

Common images of Michigan are of a major hub of the auto industry and a scenic tourist and recreational attraction, with its miles of shoreline on the Great Lakes. However, the state's Lower Peninsula is a thriving agricultural area which produces wheat, vegetables, poultry, and other goods.

Michigan's rugged Upper Peninsula has a landscape of rocky hills, rushing streams, and some 150 dramatic waterfalls.

The Great Lakes shoreline of Michigan is 3,288 miles long—longer than that of any other inland state. The chief rivers of the Upper Peninsula are the Escanaba, Manistique, Menominee, Ontonagon, Sturgeon, Tahquamenon, and Whitefish, many of which have beautiful waterfalls.

In the Lower Peninsula are the Au Sable, Clinton, Grand, Huron, Kalamazoo, St. Joseph, and other rivers. Important commercial waterways include the Detroit, St. Clair, and St. Mary's Rivers. This well-watered state has more than 11,000 lakes.

Variations in climate between the Upper and Lower Peninsulas are substantial. In the Upper Peninsula, the average January temperature is about 15 degrees Fahrenheit, and the average July temperature 64 degrees F. But Detroit, in the Lower Peninsula, has an average January temperature of 26 degrees F. and a July average of 74 degrees F. Rainfall amounts to about 30 inches annually, well dispersed through the year. Winter often brings heavy snows, especially in the Upper Peninsula, which has recorded annual snowfalls of more than 50 feet.

A picturesque winter scene on a Michigan farm. Winters are often harsh, with annual snowfall sometimes mounting to 50 feet in the Upper Peninsula.

A vest crafted by the Chippewa Indians, who were among the first inhabitants of Michigan's Upper Peninsula.

The History

When the first Europeans arrived in what was to become Michigan, some 15,000 Indians were living there—most of them belonging to tribes of the Algonquian language group. In the Upper Peninsula, the Chippewa and Menominee were the most numerous inhabitants. In the Lower Peninsula were the Miami, the Ottawa, the Potawatomi, and others. The Wyandot, members of the Iroquoian language group, lived near what is now Detroit.

Probably the first European to visit Michigan was the French explorer Étienne Brûlé, who explored the Upper Peninsula after landing at Sault Ste. Marie in 1618. He had been sent from Quebec by Samuel de Champlain, the governor of New France (now Canada). Within a few years, French fur traders and trappers were making their way to Michigan.

Champlain sent another explorer, Jean Nicolet, to the region in
1634. Nicolet was looking for a route to the Pacific Ocean, and he
sailed through the Straits of Mackinac, between the Upper and
Lower Peninsulas, and explored parts of the Upper Peninsula. In
1660 the first mission in the area was founded at Keweenaw Bay by
the Jesuit René Ménard. Eight years later Sault Ste. Marie became
Michigan's first permanent non-Indian settlement, established by the
famous explorer-priest Jacques Marquette. In 1671 another
settlement, which would become the town of St. Ignace, was
established on the northernmost point of land between Lakes
Michigan and Huron. The Indians called the place Michilimackinac.
Later it became the British Fort Mackinac because of its strategic
location.

The British built Fort
Mackinac on Mackinac
Island, between the Upper and
Lower Peninsulas, in the
1700s. Its strategic location
made it a vital military
outpost for British and, later,
American troops.

Naval commander Oliver Hazard Perry led an American flotilla to victory in the Battle of Lake Erie, during the War of 1812, thus restoring U.S. control of Lake Erie and the area around it. When Perry's ship, the *Lawrence*, was disabled in the engagement, he transferred his flag to the *Niagara* and compelled the British to surrender. This was the occasion of his famous message, "We have met the enemy and they are ours."

For the French, the lure of the Michigan forest was furs, and within a few years the annual shipment of pelts exceeded 200,000. By 1700 the French had built forts, missions, and trading posts at several places in both peninsulas. In 1701 Fort Pontchartrain, now the city of Detroit, was founded by Antoine Cadillac.

During this period, the British and the French were vying for control of North America. The Indians sided with the French, continuing to resist white incursions into their territory. The British were massacred at Fort Mackinac in 1763. That same year, an army of some 900 Indians, led by Chief Pontiac, besieged Detroit for nearly six months, but the rebellion fizzled out in the fall. When the French and Indian wars ended, Britain won most of the French holdings in North America.

During the Revolutionary War, which began in 1775, British troops from Detroit enlisted Indian aid to raid some American settlements. Although the war ended in 1783, when the Michigan area became part of the United States, the British did not surrender Detroit and Fort Mackinac until 1796.

What is now Michigan became part of the Northwest Territory in 1787 and of the Indiana Territory in 1800. Five years later Congress created the Territory of Michigan, which did not include the western section of the Upper Peninsula. During the War of 1812, the British recaptured Detroit and Fort Mackinac. But the Americans regained these two outposts in 1813 and 1814, respectively.

After the Erie Canal opened in 1825, linking the Great Lakes with the Atlantic Ocean, a steady stream of settlers moved into Michigan, chiefly from New England and New York. Michigan, including the entire Upper Peninsula, became the 26th state on January 26, 1837.

Iron-ore mining began in 1845, and many miners and prospectors came to the Upper Peninsula. When construction of the Soo Canals was completed in 1855, mine owners were able to ship ore from western Michigan to the iron and steel centers in the lower Great Lakes states.

A view of Detroit in 1820, when Michigan's population was growing rapidly as a result of territorial status and the defeat of Indian claims to the land. Five years later, completion of the Erie Canal would bring new settlers from the East.

During the Civil War, many Michiganders fought on the Union side. One of their crack units, the Fourth Michigan Cavalry, led by George Armstrong Custer, captured Confederate president Jefferson Davis in 1865.

After the Civil War, lumber became a big business in Michigan. This, in turn, fostered the furniture industry, of which Grand Rapids became the center. At the turn of the century, Michigan made its move toward becoming the automobile capital of the world when Ransom E. Olds founded the Olds Motor Works in Detroit in 1899. Oldsmobiles were being mass-produced by 1901. Two years later, Henry Ford organized the Ford Motor Company in Detroit.

When the United States entered World War I in 1917, the auto companies built trucks, armored vehicles, airplane engines, and other military products. Postwar improvements to Michigan's highway system brought many tourists to Mackinac Island and other beautiful resorts. But Michigan faced serious problems during the Great Depression of the 1930s. Hundreds of thousands of workers in the automobile industry lost their jobs, since a car was still a luxury at the time. Copper mining went into a decline because of the expense of extracting the deeply buried ore.

Automobile pioneer Henry Ford, a native of Dearborn, was instrumental in making Michigan the automobile capital of the nation. Ford's company was the first to successfully mass-produce a simple, inexpensive car that the public could afford. His four-cylinder Model T revolutionized the industry and made the Ford Motor Company one of the most successful in the world.

During World War II, Michigan reassumed its role as a center for the manufacture of airplanes, ships, tanks, and other military equipment. In fact, the entire automobile industry made nothing but these products between 1941 and 1945. Prosperity continued in the postwar years. In 1957 the great five-mile bridge across the Straits of Mackinac connected the two peninsulas. Five years later, the International Bridge to Canada opened at Sault Ste. Marie. Petroleum and natural gas reserves were developed.

Michigan's economic development has had a cyclic pattern. First there were the trees that created a great lumber industry; these were rapidly depleted. The copper and iron-ore mines followed, and they too fell into a decline. Michigan's primary mineral products today are cement, salt, crushed stone, sand, and gravel. Finally, the automobile industry, once the mainstay of the state's prosperity, has experienced difficulties with the high cost of labor and low-cost cars imported from abroad. Diversified industries like chemicals, plastics, and food have helped close the gap. The St. Lawrence Seaway made some Michigan cities international ports, which strengthened commerce, and tourism had become a $3 billion business by the early 1980s.

The St. Lawrence Seaway, completed in 1959, has played a large part in Michigan's economic prosperity. It made international ports of many Michigan cities, opening them to trade with business around the world.

Education

The first schools in Michigan were established by Roman Catholic missionaries to the Indians in the 1600s. In 1798 the first schools to teach both white and Indian children were established in Detroit by Father Gabriel Richard. The first public-school law was passed in 1809, and in 1837 a state-wide system of public education was approved by the legislature. Even before Michigan became a state in 1837, there were three institutions of higher education in the territory: the University of Michigan (1817), Kalamazoo College (1833), and Albion College (1835). When the Civil War began in 1861, six more colleges and universities had been established: Hillsdale College (1844), Olivet College (1844), Adrian College (1845), Eastern Michigan University (1849), Hope College (1851), and Michigan State University (1855). Eastern Michigan University was the first state teachers college west of New York, and Michigan State University was the first state school to offer agricultural courses for credit.

United Nations mediator and educator Ralph Bunche, the grandson of a slave, was born in Detroit and orphaned at the age of 13. His successful negotiation of agreements between Israel and the Arab states in 1949 won him the Nobel Peace Prize, awarded in 1950.

Thomas E. Dewey practiced law before he was elected governor of New York; he lost presidential campaigns to Franklin D. Roosevelt and Harry Truman.

Famous People

Many famous people were born in the state of Michigan. Here are a few:

George Allen 1922-1990, Detroit. Football coach

Avery Brundage 1887-1975, Detroit. President of the International Olympic Committee

Ralph Bunche 1904-1971, Detroit. Nobel Prize-winning diplomat

Bruce Catton 1899-1978, Petoskey. Historian

Alice Cooper b. 1948, Detroit. Rock singer

Francis Ford Coppola b. 1939, Detroit. Academy Award-winning producer-director-writer: *The Godfather, Apocalypse Now*

Dave DeBusschere b. 1940, Detroit. Hall of Fame basketball player

Thomas E. Dewey 1902-1971, Owosso. Governor and presidential candidate

John F. Dodge 1864-1920, Niles. Automobile manufacturer

Edna Ferber 1887-1968, Kalamazoo. Pulitzer Prize-winning novelist: *So Big, Giant*

Edsel Ford 1893-1943, Detroit. Automobile manufacturer

Henry Ford 1863-1947, Wayne County. Automobile manufacturer

Henry Ford II 1917-1987, Detroit. Automobile manufacturer

Harvey Fruehauf 1893-1968, Grosse Pointe Park. Truck trailer manufacturer

Frank Gerber 1873-1952, Douglas. Baby food manufacturer

Julie Harris b. 1925, Grosse Pointe. Five-time Tony Award-winning actress: *The Member of the Wedding*

Will Keith Kellogg was a cereal manufacturer who promoted cornflakes as a healthy and convenient breakfast food in the early 1900s.

James Leo Herlihy b. 1927, Detroit. Novelist: *All Fall Down, Midnight Cowboy*

Alfred D. Hershey b. 1908, Owosso. Nobel Prize-winning biologist

John Harvey Kellogg 1852-1945, Tyrone. Founded idea of mass produced healthy food in the U.S.

Will Keith Kellogg 1860-1951, Battle Creek. Cereal manufacturer

Ring Lardner 1885-1933, Niles. Short-story writer: *You Know Me, Al; Gullible's Travels*

Charles A. Lindbergh 1902-1974, Detroit. First man to fly solo across the Atlantic

Ed McMahon b. 1923, Detroit. TV announcer and host

Michael Moriarty b. 1941, Detroit. Emmy Award-winning actor: *Holocaust, The Hanoi Hilton*

Joy Morton 1855-1934, Detroit. Salt manufacturer

Della Reese b. 1931, Detroit. Jazz singer

Charles A. Lindbergh piloted the first nonstop flight from New York to Paris on The Spirit of St. Louis *in 1927.*

Sugar Ray Robinson 1921-1989, Detroit. Welterweight and middleweight boxing champion

Theodore Roethke 1908-1963, Saginaw. Pulitzer Prize-winning poet: *The Waking, Words for the Wind*

Diana Ross b. 1944, Detroit. Pop singer

Glenn Seaborg b. 1912, Ishpeming. Nobel Prize-winning chemist

Potter Stewart b. 1915, Jackson. U.S. Supreme Court justice

Danny Thomas 1914-1991, Deerfield. Comedian

Marlo Thomas b. 1943, Detroit. Television and stage actress: *That Girl, Thieves*

Lily Tomlin b. 1939, Detroit. Film actress and comedian: *Nashville, 9 to 5*

Thomas H. Weller b. 1915, Ann Arbor. Nobel Prize-winning microbiologist

Stevie Wonder b. 1950, Saginaw. Rock-blues singer

Sheila Young b. 1950, Birmingham. Olympic speed skater

Colleges and Universities

There are many colleges and universities in Michigan. Here are the more prominent, with their locations, dates of founding, and enrollments.

Adrian College, Adrian, 1859, 1,145

Albion College, Albion, 1835, 1,677

Alma College, Alma, 1886, 1,295

Aquinas College, Grand Rapids, 1886, 2,544

Calvin College, Grand Rapids, 1876, 3,725

Central Michigan University, Mount Pleasant, 1892, 16,349

Eastern Michigan University, Ypsilanti, 1849, 25,620

Ferris State College, Big Rapids, 1884, 12,461

Hillsdale College, Hillsdale, 1844, 1,080

Hope College, Holland, 1862, 2,755

Kalamazoo College, Kalamazoo, 1833, 1,245

Madonna College, Livonia, 1947, 4,419

Marygrove College, Detroit, 1910, 1,300

Michigan State University, East Lansing, 1855, 40,047

Michigan Technological University, Houghton, 1885, 6,961

Northern Michigan University, Marquette, 1899, 8,897

Oakland University, Rochester, 1957, 13,068

Siena Heights College, Adrian, 1919, 1,141

University of Detroit, Detroit, 1877, 7,774

University of Michigan, Ann Arbor, 1817, 36,626; Dearborn, 1959, 7,318; Flint, 1956, 6,652

Wayne State University, Detroit, 1868, 34,945

Western Michigan University, Kalamazoo, 1903, 27,282

Where To Get More Information

Chamber of Commerce
200 North Washington Sq.,
Suite 400
Lansing, MI 48933
or call, 1-800-543-2937

Ohio

The Seal of Ohio was adopted in 1868 and revised in 1967. It is circular and features a bundle of 17 arrows on the left (symbolizing Ohio's admission to the Union as the 17th state) and a sheaf of wheat on the right (standing for the richness of Ohio's land). Above them is the sun rising behind Mount Logan, commemorating Ohio's distinction as the first state west of the Allegheny Mountains. On the outer rim of the seal is "The Great Seal of the State of Ohio."

ONTARIO

MICHIGAN

LAKE ERIE

Toledo

Sandusky • Lorain • **Cleveland**
• Elyria

Warren •

Akron • **Youngstown**

• Findlay

• **Canton**

• Lima

Mansfield •

Marion •

NEW PHILADELPHIA ■

OHIO

Steubenville •

■
FORT RECOVERY

Newark •

Upper Arlington • ★ **Columbus** • Whitehall

Zanesville •

Springfield •

WAYNE
NATIONAL
FOREST

Dayton •

• Xenia

Lancaster •

WAYNE
NATIONAL
FOREST

• Hamilton

Chillicothe •

WAYNE
NATIONAL
FOREST

WEST VIRGINIA

Cincinnati
• Covington

INDIANA

PENNSYLVANIA

WAYNE
NATIONAL
FOREST

Portsmouth •

N
△

Ashland •

Ohio River

KENTUCKY

★ State Capital
• Cities or towns
■ OF SPECIAL INTEREST

0 10 20 30 40 50 60 Miles
0 10 20 30 40 50 60 70 80   100 Kilometres

OHIO
At a Glance

State Flag

Capital: Columbus

Major Industries: Transportation equipment, machinery, metal products

Major Crops: Corn, hay, winter wheat, oats, soybeans

State Bird: Cardinal

State Flower: Scarlet Carnation

Size: 41,330 square miles (35th largest)
Population: 11,016,385 (7th largest)

63

State Flag

The state flag of Ohio is pennant-shaped. On a background of five stripes (three red and two white) is a triangle. In the triangle is a white circle (standing for O, the state's initial) with a red center (standing for the buckeye nut). Also on the triangle are 17 stars, since Ohio was the 17th state.

State Motto

With God, All Things Are Possible

This motto, which was adopted in 1959, comes from the Bible (Matthew 19:26).

Germantown preserves many of the structures of Columbus's largest nineteenth-century ethnic group.

State Capital

The first capital of Ohio was Chillicothe (1803-10). Then came Zanesville (1810-12), and Chillicothe again (1812-16). In 1817, the state legislature voted to relocate the capital in Columbus, which had no name at the time.

State Name and Nicknames

In 1680, the French explorer Robert Cavelier, Sieur de la Salle, noted that the Iroquois Indians called the large river on the southern boundary of the area "Ohio," which meant "large [or] beautiful river." The state was then named after the river.

The most common nickname for Ohio is the *Buckeye State,* partly because of the many buckeye trees in the state and partly because of an incident that occurred in 1788. One of the colonial commanders, Colonel Sproat, was so tall that the Indians called him "Big Buckeye." Ohio is also referred to as the *Mother of Modern Presidents,* because seven U.S. presidents were born in the state.

State Flower

The scarlet carnation (family *Caryophyllaceae*) was adopted as Ohio's state flower in 1904 in memory of former President William McKinley, who thought of the flower as a good luck charm.

State Tree

In 1953, the buckeye tree, *Aesculus glabra,* was named state tree. The buckeye got its name from Indians, who thought the seed of the tree looked like the eye of the buck, or "hetuck." Other names for the tree are Ohio buckeye, fetid buckeye, stinking buckeye, and American horse chestnut.

State Bird

The cardinal, *Cardinalis cardinalis,* was designated the state bird in 1933.

State Animal

The white-tailed deer, *Odocoileus virginianus,* was adopted as the state animal in 1988.

State Insect

The Ladybird Beetle or common ladybug, was named state insect in 1975.

State Beverage

Tomato juice was named state beverage in 1965.

State Gem

Ohio flint was adopted as state gem in 1965.

State Song

"Beautiful Ohio" was adopted as the state song in 1969. It was written in 1918 by Ballard MacDonald, with music by Robert S. King. In 1989, the Ohio legislature adopted an amendment of the Ohio Revised Code that changed the words of the state song. The new lyrics are by Wilbert McBride.

Population

The population of Ohio in 1992 was 11,016,385, making it the seventh most populous state. There are 269 persons per square mile.

Industries

The principal industries of the state of Ohio are manufacturing and trade. The chief manufactured products are transportation equipment, machinery, and metal products. Other products are iron, steel, rubber, automobiles, heavy machinery, electrical and electronic components and appliances, chemicals, plastic, glass, pottery and clay products.

Agriculture

The chief crops of the state are corn, hay, winter wheat, oats, and soybeans. Ohio is also a livestock state; there are estimated to be some 1.6 million cattle, 1.9 million hogs and pigs, 24.9 million boilers, and 5 million turkeys on its farms. Oak, ash, maple, walnut, and beech trees are cut. Crushed stone, sand, gravel, lime, clays, and cement are important mineral resources. Commercial fishing earned $2.6 million in 1992.

Government

The governor, lieutenant governor, secretary-of-state, auditor, attorney general and treasurer of Ohio are all elected to four-year terms. The state legislature, which meets in odd-numbered years, currently consists of a 33-member senate and a 99-member house of representatives, though the total number of senators and representatives is not specified in the state constitution. Senators are elected to four-year terms and representatives to two-year terms. In addition to its two U.S. senators, Ohio has 19 representatives in the U.S. House of Representatives. The state has 21 votes in the electoral college. The most recent state constitution was adopted in 1851.

Sports

Ohio has always been a hotbed of sports. The first professional baseball team—the Cincinnati Red Stockings—was formed in 1869. On the collegiate level, Ohio State and the University of Cincinnati have won NCAA national basketball championships. In collegiate football, Ohio State, a perennial football power, has made many post-season bowl appearances. On the professional level, the Cincinnati Reds of the National League play baseball in Riverfront Stadium, and the Cincinnati Bengals of the National Football League share the facility. The Cleveland Indians of the American League play baseball in Cleveland Stadium. They share the facility with the Cleveland Browns of the National Football League. The Cleveland Cavaliers of the National Basketball Association play in the Coliseum in nearby Richfield.

Major Cities

Cincinnati (population 364,114). Settled in 1788, it was originally called Losantiville. During the early 1800s, many immigrants moved in, most of them Germans. Cincinnati was soon to become a bustling frontier riverboat town. Today it is a city with charm, culture, and fine food.

Things to see in Cincinnati: Cincinnati Zoo and Botanical Garden, Carew Tower, Hamilton County Courthouse, Public Landing, City Hall (1888), William Howard Taft National Historic Site, Harriet Beecher Stowe Memorial, John Hauck House Museum, Loveland Castle, Contemporary Arts Center, Cincinnati Fire Museum, Taft Museum (1820), Mount Airy Forest and

A view of the brilliantly-lit skyline of Cincinnati, the state's third-largest metropolitan area.

Arboretum, Civic Garden Center of Greater Cincinnati, Mount Adams, Museum of Natural History and Planetarium, Cincinnati Art Museum, and Sharon Woods Village.

Cleveland (population 505,616). Founded in 1796 by Moses Cleveland, the town soon began to profit from Great Lakes transportation, and later became a bustling industrial town. Today, Ohio's most populous city still retains the charm of wide streets, 39 city parks and 17,500 acres of metropolitan parks.

Things to see in Cleveland:
City Hall, Federal Buildings, Public Square, USS *Cod*, Dunham Tavern Museum, Cleveland Health Education Museum, Lake View Cemetery, Cleveland Museum of Art, Cleveland Museum of Natural History, Ralph Mueller Planetarium, the Western Reserve Historical Society Museum and Library, Frederick C. Crawford Auto-Aviation Museum, Wade Park and Garden Center, Cultural Gardens, Rockefeller

Greenhouse, Temple Museum of Religious Art, Dittrick Museum of Medical History, Cleveland Metroparks Zoo, and NASA Lewis Visitor Center.

Columbus (population 632,945). Founded in 1812, Columbus was created and laid out to be the capital of Ohio. By 1833, the new National Road reached the town and it began to grow. Today, it is a most attractive city, with broad tree-lined streets and beautiful parks.

Things to see in Columbus:
Ohio State Capitol, McKinley Memorial, City Hall, Camp Chase Confederate Cemetery, Ohio Historical Center, Ohio Village, Ohio's Center of Science and Industry, Columbus Museum of Art, Ohio Railway Museum, German Village, Columbus Zoological Gardens, Park of Roses, Chadwick Arboretum, and Franklin Park Conservatory and Garden Center.

Places to Visit
The National Park Service maintains four areas in the

state of Ohio: Mound City Group National Monument, Perry's Victory and International Peace Memorial, William Howard Taft Birthplace, and Wayne National Forest. In addition, there are 65 state recreation areas.

Akron: Stan Hywet Hall and Gardens. This Tudor revival

Cleveland's location on Lake Erie helped make it a major industrial city.

Canton is home to the Professional Football Hall of Fame, where visitors can learn the history of the game and see its great collection of memorabilia.

mansion, with 65 rooms, contains antiques and art treasures.

Ashtabula: Great Lakes Marine and U.S. Coast Guard Memorial Museum. Many maritime exhibits are displayed in the 1898 lighthouse keeper's home.

Aurora: Sea World. This marine-life park has regular shows, with killer whales, dolphins, seals, and sea otters.

Bowling Green: Educational Memorabilia Center. More than 1,500 historic educational items are displayed in a restored one-room schoolhouse.

Canton: Pro Football Hall of Fame. Thousands of items of professional football memorabilia are on display here.

Coshocton: Roscoe Village Restoration. This restoration of a busy town on the Ohio-Erie Canal, settled in 1816, includes the Toll House with model locks.

Dayton: Wright Cycle Shop. This is a replica of the shop where the Wright Brothers performed their experiments

in aviation. United States Air Force Museum.

Defiance: Au Glaize Village. Replicas and restored 19th-century buildings include a railroad station with rolling stock.

Delaware: Olentangy Indian Caverns and Ohio Frontierland. This is a natural limestone cave and Indian village.

Mansfield: Kingwood Center and Gardens. Here are 49 acres of landscaped gardens and greenhouses.

Marietta: Campus Martius and Museum of the Northwest Territory. Historic buildings from the 1700s.

Marion: President Warren G. Harding's Home and Museum.

Mason: Kings Island. This 1600-acre family entertainment center contains a zoo and more than 40 rides.

New Philadelphia: Zoar State Memorial. The quaint village, where German religious separatists sought refuge in 1817, was an experiment in communal living for 80 years.

Sandusky: Cedar Point. An amusement park with 54 rides and live shows near a mile-long beach and marina.

Springfield: Westcott House. This 1908 home was designed by Frank Lloyd Wright.

Strongsville: Gardenview Horticultural Park. Here are 16 acres of English-style gardens with rare plants.

Toledo: Toledo Zoological Gardens. More than 2,000 animals are on display here.

Wapakoneta: Neil Armstrong Air and Space Museum. Aircraft including balloons and the Gemini 8 capsule in which Armstrong accomplished the first spacecraft docking in orbit are displayed here.

Warren: John Stark Edwards House. Built in 1807, this is the oldest house in the Western Reserve.

Wauseon: Sauder Farm and Craft Village. Farmstead and pioneer village with craft demonstrations.

Events

There are many events and organizations that schedule activities of various kinds in the state of Ohio. Here are some of them.

Sports: All-American Soapbox Derby (Akron); NEC "World Series of Golf" (Akron); National Jigsaw Puzzle Championship (Athens); National Tractor Pulling Championship (Bowling Green); International Chicken Flying Meet (Gallipolis); Four Wheeler Rodeo (Lisbon); Ohio Ski Carnival (Mansfield); auto racing at Mid-Ohio Sports Car Course (Mansfield); National Archery Tournament (Oxford); National Matches (Port Clinton); Charity Horse Show (Portsmouth); Grand American Tournament of the Amateur Trapshooting Association of America (Vandalia).

Arts and Crafts: Carnation Festival (Alliance); Ohio Hills Folk Festival (Cambridge); Salt Forks Arts and Crafts Festival (Cambridge); Tri-State Pottery Festival (East Liverpool); Zane Square Arts and Crafts Festival (Lancaster); Square Fair/Summer Community Arts Festival (Lima); Indian Summer Arts and Crafts Festival (Marietta).

Music: Ohio Ballet (Akron); Akron Symphony (Akron); Blossom Music Center (Akron); Canton Symphony (Canton); Canton Ballet (Canton); Canton Civic Opera (Canton); Cincinnati Ballet Company (Cincinnati); Cincinnati Opera Association (Cincinnati); Cincinnati Symphony (Cincinnati); May Festival (Cincinnati); Riverfront Stadium Festival (Cincinnati);

The rollercoaster loops of Cedar Point are only one attraction at the amusement park in Sandusky.

Cleveland Ballet (Cleveland); Cleveland Opera (Cleveland); Cleveland Orchestra (Cleveland); Ballet Met (Columbus); Stuart Pimsler Dance and Theater (Columbus); Opera/Columbus (Columbus); Columbus Symphony (Columbus); Greater Columbus Arts Festival (Columbus); Dulcimer Days (Coshocton); Dayton Philharmonic (Dayton); Concerts at the Dayton Art Institute (Dayton); Summer Series of Concerts (Dayton); Zivili Kolo Ensemble (Granville); US Open Drum and Bugle Corps Competition (Marion); Jamboree in the Hills (St. Clairsville); Toledo Symphony (Toledo); Youngstown Symphony (Youngstown).

Entertainment: Train Meet (Akron); Wonderful World of Ohio Mart (Akron); Harvest Festival (Akron); Cherry Festival (Bellevue); Bratwurst Festival (Bucyrus); Celina Lake Festival (Celina); Geauga County Maple Festival (Chardon); Fall Festival of Leaves (Chillicothe); Riverfest (Cincinnati); International Folk Festival (Cincinnati); Ohio State Fair (Columbus); Columbus Day Celebration (Columbus); Coshocton Canal Festival (Coshocton); River Festival (Dayton); Dayton Air and Trade Show (Dayton); Flowing Rivers Festival (Defiance); Geneva Grape Jamboree (Geneva-on-the-Lake); Fort Hamilton Days Festival (Hamilton); Antique Car Parade (Hamilton); Tri-State Fair and Regatta (Ironton); Spring Old Car Festival (Lancaster); Lancaster Festival (Lancaster); Ohio Honey Festival (Lebanon); Johnny Appleseed Festival (Lisbon); International Festival Week (Lorain); Ohio River Sternwheel Festival (Marietta); Popcorn Festival (Marion); Zoar Harvest Festival (New Philadelphia); Swiss Festival (New Philadelphia); Heritage Festival (Piqua); Roy Rogers Convention and Western Festival (Portsmouth); Portsmouth Sternwheel Regatta and Festival (Portsmouth); River Days Festival (Portsmouth); International Festival (Toledo); Northwest Ohio Rib-Off (Toledo); Fall Folk Festival (Toledo); Zane's Trace Commemoration (Zanesville).

Tours: Pilgrimage Tour of 19th-Century homes (Lancaster); Christmas Candlelight Tours (Lancaster); Hocking Hills Fall Color Caravan Tour (Logan).

Theater: Ohio Valley Summer Theater (Athens); The Living Word Outdoor Drama (Cambridge); "Tecumseh!"

The Pumpkin Festival in Circleville is a fall tradition.

Tecumseh! *is an outdoor drama production in Chillicothe, a town that takes its name from Chahlagawtha, a Shawnee village that occupied that site.*

Sailboats navigate the placid waters of Lake Erie, which forms part of the northern border of Ohio.

(Chillicothe); Cincinnati Playhouse in the Park (Cincinnati); Cleveland Play House (Cleveland); Actors Summer Theater (Columbus); Lakewood Little Theater (Lakewood); Showboat Becky Thatcher (Marietta); "Trumpet in the Land" (New Philadelphia); Youngstown Playhouse (Youngstown).

The Land and the Climate

Ohio is bounded on the west by Indiana, on the north by Michigan and Lake Erie, on the east by Pennsylvania and West Virginia, and on the south by West Virginia and Kentucky. There are four main land regions in the state, formed primarily by the Ice Age glaciers. They are the Great Lakes Plains, the Till Plains, the Appalachian Plateau, and the Bluegrass Region.

The Great Lakes Plains lie along the northern border of Ohio and are part of a larger area that borders the Great Lakes. These level plains are broken by a few low sandy ridges along Lake Erie. The region has fertile soil, and fruits and vegetables are its chief crops. It is also a populous area of large cities, lake ports, and industrial complexes.

The Till Plains, part of the great Midwestern Corn Belt, are located in western Ohio. There are some hills here in what is one of the nation's most fertile farming areas. Grain and livestock are raised in the Till Plains, which also contain a few industrial cities.

While much of Ohio is highly industrialized, agriculture remains an important part of the state's economy. Many of the largest farms can be found in the northwest and central portions of the state.

Southwestern Ohio is an extension of the Kentucky Bluegrass Region. This area is well suited to horse raising and the cultivation of tobacco, corn, and wheat.

The Appalachian Plateau is located in eastern Ohio. The southern part of the area, the only section not glaciated, is rugged country, where most of the soil is not suitable for farming. But in the north, the soil produces both crops and good pasturage for dairy cows.

The Bluegrass Region is a small triangular area in southwestern Ohio that extends from Kentucky's Bluegrass Region. Tobacco is grown here. Corn, wheat, and beef cattle are other farm products of the region.

Ohio's shoreline extends for 312 miles along Lake Erie. The state has some 44,000 miles of rivers and streams, of which the Ohio is the most important. Other major waterways are the Miami, Hocking, Muskingum, Scioto, Cayahoga, Maumee, Sandusky, and Vermilion Rivers. Ohio has more than 2,500 lakes with an area larger than two acres.

Ohio's climate is continental, or mid-American, with from 35 to 39 inches of rainfall throughout the year, fairly well distributed over the state. Cleveland, in the north, has an average January temperature of 28 degrees Fahrenheit and a July average of 71 degrees F. Cincinnati, in the south, has a January average of 33 degrees F. and a July average of 76 degrees F. In the snow belt along the shore of Lake Erie, heavy winter snowfalls are likely to occur. The Cincinnati area has the state's hottest summer weather.

Southeastern Ohio has a rugged landscape dotted with many small rivers and lakes, including Lake Vesuvius, seen here.

The History

Paleo-Indians lived in what is now Ohio more than 5,000 years ago. Later groups, known to us as Mound Builders, left more than 6,000 burial mounds, forts, and other earthworks throughout the state, the products of a high form of civilization. These cultures flourished from about 1400 B.C. to A.D. 500.

The first Europeans to arrive encountered the Delaware, Miami, Shawnee, Huron (or Wyandot), and other tribes. The first non-Indian to visit the Ohio area was probably the French explorer Robert Cavelier (La Salle), who arrived in 1670. The French based their claim to the entire Northwest on his explorations. The British also claimed these lands, which they viewed as extensions of their Eastern colonies. The British Ohio Company of Virginia sent Christopher Gist to explore the upper Ohio River Valley in 1750, with a view toward colonizing the area. British soldiers and explorers from the Atlantic Seaboard colonies built wilderness garrisons (some of which would become cities) and held the land against the French in a long series of struggles—the French and Indian Wars—that ended in 1763. France gave up its claims to all lands as far west as the Mississippi River in a treaty signed that year.

A Moravian religious settlement named Schoenbrunn, near present-day New Philadelphia, had been established in 1772. But it disbanded a few years later because of Revolutionary War battles nearby. In 1780 George Rogers Clark defeated Indian allies of the British in the Battle of Piqua, near what is now Springfield. Clark's frontier campaigns helped win the region for the United States.

After the American Revolution, Ohio was included in the Northwest Territory (roughly the present area of the Midwest), and settlement began. The first permanent non-Indian settlement was at Marietta, near the Ohio River, in 1788. Cincinnati was founded the same year. The area began to fill with settlers, as Revolutionary War

Revolutionary War hero General Rufus Putnam was superintendent of the Ohio Company of Associates, a group formed in the late 1780s to purchase large tracts of land in the Ohio country. The company bought 1,500,000 acres in southeastern Ohio for about 75 cents per acre and founded the state's first permanent non-Indian settlement, the town of Marietta.

veterans received its land in payment for their services. The Indians had resisted encroachments on their territory since the 1760s, when Chief Pontiac led an unsuccessful uprising against the British. After the Revolution, resistance continued under the leadership of Miami chief Little Turtle and others. General Anthony Wayne dealt a death blow to the Indian cause at the Battle of Fallen Timbers, near present-day Toledo, in 1794.

Twelve years after the first settlement, and three years before Ohio became a state, the area had a population of more than 45,000— chiefly immigrants from New England, Pennsylvania, and Kentucky. Among them was a man named John Chapman, whose nickname was "Johnny Appleseed." His passion for orchards gave the fields cut from the forests a springtime pattern of flowering trees, and still gives Ohio a high rank among apple-producing states.

Ohio became the 17th state in the Union in 1803, with Chillicothe as its capital. The capital was moved to Zanesville in 1810, then back to Chillicothe in 1812. Finally, Columbus became the capital in 1816.

During the War of 1812 with Great Britain, one of the most important battles took place off the Ohio shore on Lake Erie. Commodore Oliver H. Perry sailed from Put-in-Bay at South Bass Island to defeat the British fleet in the Battle of Lake Erie on September 10, 1813.

The Erie Canal across New York from Lake Erie opened in 1825, offering a new and easy route for settlement of Ohio and the West. Thousands of families moved in from northern New York and New England. European immigrants, especially Germans, arrived in great numbers, and by 1830 there were almost a million people in the state. Transportation continued to improve with completion of the Ohio and Erie Canal from Cleveland to Portsmouth in 1832. And the Miami and Erie Canal from Toledo to Cincinnati opened in 1845. Railroads reached Ohio from the East, increasing population and prosperity. Mills and factories were built.

The city of Cleveland in 1850. The mid-19th century was a time of great growth for Ohio, particularly in the north, where successful drainage projects opened up new land for farming.

Ohioans had mixed feelings about the issue of slavery: many were active abolitionists, while others sympathized with the South. But during the Civil War, which began in 1861, some 345,000 men responded to Union calls for volunteers—more than twice the state's quota. Ohio also provided the Union's key commanders: Generals Ulysses S. Grant, William T. Sherman, and Philip H. Sheridan. The only important military action within Ohio during the Civil War occurred when Confederate cavalrymen called Morgan's Raiders crossed into the state from Indiana. They were captured with their leader, General John Hunt Morgan, in Columbiana County, but Morgan escaped later and returned to the South.

Morgan's Raid, in 1863, was the only major penetration into Ohio by Confederate troops during the Civil War. After the unsuccessful attack, Confederate cavalry leader John Hunt Morgan and his men were imprisoned.

After the Civil War ended, Ohio's abundant natural resources and its strategic position between two of the country's principal waterways—Lake Erie on the north and the Ohio River on the south—paved the way for rapid industrialization and growth. Shipping and farming increased. In 1869 the Cincinnati Red Stockings (now the Reds) became the first professional baseball team, and rubber-products production was started in Akron by Benjamin F. Goodyear in 1870.

During World War I, which the United States entered in 1917, about 225,000 Buckeyes served in the armed forces, and the state produced vast amounts of war materials. The 1920s were a time of growth in Ohio, as many towns became cities, and barges loaded with coal and iron ore plied Lake Erie. But when the Great Depression of the 1930s began, many factory workers became unemployed as a result of plant closings. Ohio farmers lost their land when farm prices dropped.

Harvey Firestone, born in Columbiana, Ohio, founded the Firestone Tire and Rubber Company in Akron in 1900. The balloon tire he produced soon became an industry standard, and his successful business provided employment for thousands of Ohio workers.

During World War II, about 840,000 Ohioans were in the armed forces. Steel, tires, and other goods needed for the military made Ohio one of the top four states in contracts awarded for wartime industries. Aircraft, ships, and weapons rolled from Ohio assembly lines.

After the war ended in 1945, Ohio became one of the most important states in the development of atomic energy for peacetime use. The Ohio Turnpike, opened in 1955, stretched across the 241-mile width of northern Ohio. In 1970 during protests against U.S. military action in Cambodia, four Kent State University students were fatally shot by National Guardsmen. This incident heightened college campus tensions throughout the United States.

Today, Ohio's industrial growth is still running at a strong pace. New industries are attracted by the state's four major ports, and there are international airports at Cleveland, Dayton, Cincinnati, and Columbus. Ohio has more large metropolitan areas than any other state. Ohioans are justifiably proud of their excellent state park system, their numerous tree-shaded towns, and their "Queen City," Cincinnati.

Education

The first school in Ohio opened in 1773 at Schoenbrunn, near present-day New Philadelphia. It was set up by a Moravian missionary, David Zeisberger, to teach Indian children of the region. The public-school system of Ohio began in 1825, and public high schools were established from 1853 onward. The first institution of higher education in Ohio was Marietta College, which was founded in 1797. The second was Ohio University, which was established in 1804, just one year after statehood. Colleges and universities proliferated, and by the beginning of the Civil War in 1861, Ohio

Inventor Thomas Alva Edison was born in Milan, Ohio. His numerous inventions included the incandescent light bulb, the phonograph, and one of the first successful motion-picture cameras.

had 24 more of them, including the University of Cincinnati, the oldest municipal university in the United States founded in 1819. In 1833, Oberlin College was established and was the first coeducational college in the United States. It was also one of the first colleges to admit black students.

The People

More than 73 percent of the people of Ohio live in towns and such cities as Cleveland, Cincinnati, Columbus, Dayton, Akron, and

Markswoman Annie Oakley, born in Darke County, Ohio, in 1860, starred in Buffalo Bill's Wild West Show for 17 years.

William Tecumseh Sherman, born in Lancaster, was one of the greatest Union generals of the Civil War.

Toledo. About 95 percent of Ohioans were born in the United States. Most of those born in foreign countries came from Czechoslovakia, England, Germany, Hungary, Italy, and Poland. The largest religious group is the Roman Catholic community. Major Protestant denominations include the Disciples of Christ, Lutherans, Methodists, and Presbyterians.

Far left:
Actress Lillian Gish, a native of Springfield, became a legend of the silver screen.

At left:
Clarence Darrow, renowned criminal lawyer and social reformer, was born near Kinsman, Ohio. He won fame in 1925 for his moving defense of John T. Scopes, who was charged with, and convicted of, teaching evolution in Tennessee's public schools, in what was called the "monkey trial."

OHIO: *Mother of Presidents*

Ulysses S. Grant a renowned Union general during the Civil War and the 18th president of the United States, was born in Point Pleasant.

Rutherford B. Hayes, born in Delaware, Ohio, was the 19th president of the United States.

James A Garfield, born in Orange, the 20th president.

North Bend native Benjamin Harrison, the 23rd president.

William McKinley, the 25th president, born in Niles.

William Taft, the 27th president, born in Cincinnati.

Warren G. Harding, the 29th president, born in Blooming Grove.

Famous People

Many famous people were born in the state of Ohio. Here are a few:

Sherwood Anderson 1876-1941, Camden. Novelist: *Winesburg, Ohio; Dark Laughter*

Eddie Arcaro b. 1916, Cincinnati. Jockey

Neil Armstrong b. 1930, Wapakoneta. Astronaut

Erma Bombeck b. 1927, Dayton. Columnist

Paul Brown 1908-91, Norwalk. Hall of Fame football coach

Paul Laurence Dunbar 1872-1906, Dayton. Poet: "We Wear the Mask," "Little Brown Baley"

Arthur H. Compton 1892-1962, Wooster. Nobel Prize-winning physicist

Powel Crosley, Jr. 1886-1961, Cincinnati. Industrialist and owner of the Cincinnati Reds

Dayton native Orville Wright (left), and his brother Wilbur, who was born in Indiana, built the first successful airplane. In 1903, at Kitty Hawk, North Carolina, Orville made the first engine-powered flights in aviation history.

Far left:
John Glenn, born in Cambridge, was the first American astronaut to orbit the earth. He is now a U.S. senator from Ohio.

At left:
Astronaut Neil A. Armstrong, a native of Wapakoneta, Ohio, was the first man to set foot on the moon, in 1969.

Hart Crane 1899-1932, Garrettsville. Poet: *The Bridge, White Buildings*

George A. Custer 1839-1876, New Rumley. Union Army officer and Indian fighter

Clarence Darrow 1857-1938, near Kinsman. Lawyer

Charles G. Dawes 1865-1951, Marietta. Nobel Prize-winning diplomat

Len Dawson b. 1935, Alliance. Hall of Fame football player

Doris Day b. 1924, Cincinnati. Movie actress:

The Pajama Game, That Touch of Mink

Phyllis Diller b. 1917, Lima. Comedienne

Hugh Downs b. 1921, Akron. TV newsman

Thomas Edison 1847-1931,

Thomas Edison, who invented the light bulb and the phonograph, was granted over 1,000 patents during his life.

Milan. Inventor of the light bulb

Daniel Decatur Emmett 1815-1904, Mt. Vernon. Entertainer and songwriter

Suzanne Farrell b. 1945, Cincinnati. Ballerina

Harvey Firestone 1868-1938, Columbiana. Tire manufacturer

Clark Gable 1901-1960, Cadiz. Academy Award-winning actor: *It Happened One Night, Gone with the Wind*

James N. Gamble 1836-1932, Cincinnati. Soap manufacturer

James A. Garfield 1831-1881, near Orange. Twentieth President of the United States

John Glenn b. 1921, Cambridge. Astronaut and U.S. senator

David M. Goodrich 1876-1950, Akron. Tire manufacturer

Ulysses S. Grant 1822-1885, Point Pleasant. Eighteenth President of the United States

Joel Grey b. 1932, Cleveland. Academy Award-winning actor: *Cabaret, Remo Williams: The Adventure Begins*

Warren G. Harding 1865-1923, Blooming Grove. Twenty-ninth President of the United States

Benjamin Harrison 1833-1901, North Bend. Twenty-third President of the United States

John Havlicek b. 1940, Martins Ferry. Hall of Fame basketball player

Rutherford B. Hayes 1822-1893, Delaware. Nineteenth President of the United States

Zane Grey 1875-1939, Zanesville. Western novelist: *The Last of the*

Suzanne Farrell was a star of the New York City Ballet.

Plainsmen, Riders of the Purple Sage

Kenesaw Mountain Landis 1866-1944, Millville. Commissioner of baseball

James Levine b. 1943, Cincinnati. Opera conductor

James Lovell b. 1928, Cleveland. Astronaut

Henry Mancini b. 1924, Cleveland. Song composer

William H. Masters b. 1915, Cleveland. Sexologist

William McKinley 1843-1901, Niles. Twenty-fifth President of the United States

Toni Morrison b. 1931, Lorain. 1993 Nobel Prize Laureate for Literature: *The Song of Solomon, Beloved, Jazz*

Edwin Moses b. 1953, Dayton. Olympic gold medal-winning hurdler

Paul Newman b. 1925, Cleveland. Academy Award-winning actor: *The*

Color of Money, The Verdict

Jack Nicklaus b. 1940, Columbus. Championship golfer

Ransom E. Olds 1864-1950, Geneva. Auto manufacturer

James W. Packard 1863-1928, Warren. Auto manufacturer

Norman Vincent Peale b. 1898, Bowersville. Clergyman

Tyrone Power 1914-1958, Cincinnati. Film actor: *The Sun Also Rises, Witness for the Prosecution*

Sally Priesand b. 1946, Cleveland. First American woman rabbi

William Proctor 1862-1934, Glendale. Soap manufacturer

Charles F. Richter 1900-1985, near Hamilton. Seismologist and developer of the Richter Scale

Eddie Rickenbacker 1890-1973, Columbus. World War I air ace

Branch Rickey 1881-1965, Stockdale. Hall of Fame baseball executive

John D. Rockefeller, Jr. 1874-1960, Cleveland. Philanthropist

Roy Rogers b. 1912, Cincinnati. Film cowboy star

Pete Rose b. 1941, Cincinnati. Baseball player and manager

Arthur Schlesinger b. 1917, Columbus. Historian

Martin Sheen b. 1940, Dayton. Film actor: *Apocalypse Now, The Dead Zone*

William Tecumseh Sherman 1820-1891, Lancaster. Union general

Roger Staubach b. 1942, Cincinnati. Hall of Fame football quarterback

Gloria Steinem b. 1934, Toledo. Feminist writer

William Howard Taft 1857-1930, Cincinnati. Twenty-seventh President of the United States and chief justice of the Supreme Court

Art Tatum 1910-1956, Toledo. Jazz pianist

Tecumseh 1768-1813, Greene County. Shawnee Indian chief

Norman Thomas 1884-1968, Marion. Co-founder of the American Civil Liberties Union

James Thurber 1894-1961, Columbus. Humorist: *My Life and Hard Times, The Years with Ross*

Ted Turner b. 1938, Cincinnati. Communications executive

Paul Warfield b. 1942, Warren. Hall of Fame football player

Jonathan Winters b. 1925, Dayton. Television and film comedian: *The Loved One, Viva Max*

Victoria Woodhull 1838-1927, Homer. First woman candidate for president

Orville Wright 1871-1948, Dayton. Co-developer of the airplane

Cy Young 1867-1955, Gilmore. Hall of Fame baseball pitcher

Colleges and Universities

There are many colleges and universities in Ohio. Here are the more prominent, with their locations, dates of founding, and enrollments.

Ashland College, Ashland, 1878, 5,652

Cy Young won more games (511) than any other major-league pitcher.

Baldwin-Wallace College, Berea, 1845, 4,736

Bowling Green State University, Bowling Green, 1910, 17,502

Capital University, Columbus, 1850, 3,680

Case Western Reserve University, Cleveland, 1826, 9,156

Central State University, Wilberforce, 1887, 3,279

Cleveland State University, Cleveland, 1964, 18,199

College of Mount St. Joseph, Cincinnati, 1920, 2,592

College of Wooster, Wooster, 1866, 1,686

Denison University, Granville, 1831, 2,003

Heidelberg College, Tiffin, 1850, 1,182

John Carroll University, University Heights, 1886, 4,488

Kent State University, Kent, 1910, 24,100

Kenyon College, Gambier, 1824, 1,488

Marietta College, Marietta, 1835, 1,379

Miami University, Oxford, 1809, 16,104

Mount Union College, Alliance, 1846, 1,410

Muskingum College, New Concord, 1837, 1,135

Oberlin College, Oberlin, 1833, 2,902

Ohio Northern University, Ada, 1871, 2,872

The Ohio State University, Columbus, 1870, 52,183; Lima, 1960, 1,410; Mansfield, 1958, 1,465; Marion, 1957, 1,066; Newark, 1957, 1,732

Ohio University, Athens, 1804, 18,248; Chillicothe, 1946, 1,738; Ironton, 1956, 1,477; Lancaster, 1968, 1,554; Zanesville, 1946, 1,232

Ohio Wesleyan University, Delaware, 1842, 2,037

Otterbein College, Westerville, 1847, 2,531

University of Akron, Akron, 1870, 27,079

University of Cincinnati, Cincinnati, 1819, 17,931

University of Dayton, Dayton, 1850, 10,658

University of Toledo, Toledo, 1872, 24,541

Ursuline College, Cleveland, 1871, 1,600

Wittenberg University, Springfield, 1845, 2,250

Wright State University, Dayton, 1964, 17,657

Xavier University, Cincinnati, 1831, 6,383

Youngstown State University, Youngstown, 1908, 14,806

Where To Get More Information

Chamber of Commerce
35 East Gay Street
Columbus, OH 43215
or call, 1-800-BUCKEYE

Further Reading

General

Aylesworth, Thomas G., and Virginia L. Aylesworth. *State Reports: The Eastern Great Lakes: Indiana, Michigan, Ohio.* New York: Chelsea House, 1991.

Indiana

Aylesworth, Thomas G., and Virginia L. Aylesworth. *Indiana.* Greenwich, CT: Bison Books, 1985.

Dillion, Lowell I., and E. E. Lyon, eds. *Indiana: Crossroads of America.* Dubuque, IA: Kendall/Hunt, 1978.

Esarey, Logan. *A History of Indiana.* 2 vols. in one. Indianapolis: Hoosier Heritage Press, 1970.

Hoover, Dwight W., and Jane Rodman. *A Pictorial History of Indiana.* Bloomington: Indiana University Press, 1981.

Nolan, Jeanette. *Indiana.* New York: Coward, McCann & Geoghegan, 1969.

Peckham, Howard H. *Indiana: A Bicentennial History.* New York: Norton, 1978.

Stein, P. Conrad. *America the Beautiful: Indiana.* Chicago: Childrens Press, 1990.

Wilson, William E. *Indiana: A History.* Bloomington: Indiana University Press, 1966.

Michigan

Bailey, Bernadine. *Picture Book of Michigan,* rev. ed. Chicago: Whitman, 1967.

Catton, Bruce. *Michigan: A History.* New York: Norton, 1984.

Dunbar, Willis F. *Michigan: A History of the Wolverine State,* rev. ed. Grand Rapids, MI: Eerdman, 1980.

Fradin, Dennis B. *From Sea to Shining Sea: Michigan.* Chicago: Childrens Press, 1992.

Stein, P. Conrad. *America the Beautiful: Michigan.* Chicago: Childrens Press, 1987.

Ohio

Collins, William R. *Ohio: The Buckeye State,* 6th ed. Englewood Cliffs, NJ: Prentice Hall, 1980.

Croul, George C. , and W. E. Rosenfelt. *Ohio: Its People and Culture.* Minneapolis, MN: Denison, 1977.

Fradin, Dennis B. *From Sea to Shining Sea: Ohio.* Chicago: Childrens Press, 1993.

Havinghurst, Walter. *Ohio: A Bicentennial History.* New York: Norton, 1976.

Kent, Deborah. *America the Beautiful: Ohio.* Chicago: Childrens Press, 1989.

Roseboom, Eugene H., and Francis P. Weisenburger. *A History of Ohio.* 2nd ed. Columbus: Ohio Historical Society, 1984.

Numbers in italics refer to illustrations

Photo Credits

Courtesy of Terry Cartwright: pp. 42-43; Courtesy of David J. Castelli: p. 68; Courtesy of Dave Giorgis: p. 73 (bottom); Courtesy of the Indiana Department of Commerce: pp. 3 (top), 6, 7, 8-9, 11, 12, 13, 14, 15, 16, 17, 18, 19, 21, 24 (bottom), 25, 26, 30; Courtesy of the Indiana Historical Bureau: p. 5; Courtesy of Kellogg Company: p. 38 (right); James Kersell: p. 63 (top left); Library of Congress: pp. 24 (top), 55, 77, 80, 84 (left), 85 (right), 88; Courtesy of Metropolitan Detroit Convention & Visitors Bureau: p. 40; Courtesy of Michigan Travel Bureau: pp. 3 (bottom), 31, 32-33, 34-35, 37, 38, 39, 42, 43, 44, 45, 46-47, 48, 49, 51, 56; Museum of the American Indian: p. 50; NASA: pp. 27 (top), 89; Courtesy of the National Baseball Library: p. 92; National Portrait Gallery: pp. 23, 27 (bottom), 52, 57, 81, 83, 84 (right), 86, 87; Courtesy of New York City Ballet: p. 90 (bottom); New York Public Library/Stokes Collection: pp. 54, 79; Courtesy of New York Public Library Picture Collection: pp. 29, 90 (top); Courtesy of the Ohio Division of Travel and Tourism: pp. 4, 61, 69, 70, 71, 72, 73 (top), 74, 75; Courtesy of the State Archives of Michigan: pp. 58 (left), 59.
Cover photos courtesy of Dave Giorgis; Indiana Department of Commerce; and Michigan Travel Bureau.